T0064835

Skippering a Small Keelboat

SKILLS FROM THE MASTERS

Modern Lessons From the Fastest-Growing Global Sailing Education and Certification Program

GRANT HEADIFEN

Seahorse Publishing

Dedication

To the love of my life, my daughter Alexandra. Her strong, free spirit is a perfect match for the wind and the ocean.

Acknowledgments

Many of the photos in this book are courtesy of Beneteau.

A big thanks to Lauren Zykorie for her untiring editing efforts and for bringing me back to the basics. Her queries of "Huh? What the heck does this mean?" allowed me to make this book understandable for the new sailor.

Copyright © 2016 by Grant Headifen

Skyhorse Publishing books may be purchased in bulk at special discounts for sales promotion, corporate gifts, fund-raising, or educational purposes. Special editions can also be created to specifications. For details, contact the Special Sales Department, Skyhorse Publishing, 307 West 36th Street, 11th Floor, New York, NY 10018or info@skyhorsepublishing.com.

Skyhorse® and Skyhorse Publishing® are registered trademarks of Skyhorse Publishing, Inc.®, a Delaware corporation.

Visit our website at www.skyhorsepublishing.com.

10 9 8 7 6 5 4 3 2 1

Library of Congress Cataloging-in-Publication Data is available on file.

Cover design by Tom Lau
Cover photo credit Annapolis Boat Sales

Print ISBN: 978-1-944824-04-4

Printed in China

Contents

Introduction

Grant Headifen.

How this book works

This book is unlike any other book you've read. We call it a hybrid eBook. While the book can stand alone on it's own as one of the best learn-to-sail books written, it also employs some really cool technology should you decide to take advantage.

Throughout the book, you will see QR codes. When you scan these codes with your mobile device, the book will come alive and present interactive animations, videos and useful websites. This will vastly enhance your learning experience.

To get a QR code reader, simply search on any App store. QR code readers are free. Alternatively, NauticEd also provides a free iOS App that can read QR codes. You can go to www.NauticEd.org/sailing-apps and download the free app there. Once you have it downloaded, click on the hybrid eBook link in the App menu.

Try out your QR Code reader now and go to the webpage (http://www.nauticed.org/book-sskb) for this book where we show an introductory video, all the links used for this book, and any updates post publication.

NauticEd is one of the world's leading premier sailing training companies and the only company to employ super high technology systems into its training programs. NauticEd also helps students gain the ICC, the International Certificate of Competence. The ICC was created by United Nations and is required as a sailing license in many countries. Yacht charter companies worldwide accept the NauticEd sailing resume and certification system.

This book then, is not only going to be part of your world class sailing training but will lead you to a highly regarded sailing certification; one that is accepted globally.

As part of your purchase of this book, you will also have free access to a lot of tools that are introduced in this book. You'll simply scan the QR codes and a new world of modern sailing training, sailing resumes, sailing logbooks and sailing badges will be opened to you; ALL FOR FREE.

About this course

This is a fun course for beginner-to-intermediate sailors on sailboats around the 22-foot (6.5 m) range, though experienced sailors will also pick up some gems, as well. We've also taken a unique approach to sailing education: we've made it fun. We tell little stories, crack jokes, and use an informal style of language you'll appreciate. It's in my nature; everyone goes sailing to have fun (that is, since the invention of the engine). So why not have fun while learning how to sail? With that said, however, we are serious about burning into your brain the necessary knowledge you need to have to be a great sailor.

This course presents the theory of learning to sail only (ha ha, obviously). But, as you will soon recognize, theoretical knowledge is as important as practical expertise. Case in point: who gives way in the crossing situation on the next page?

You simply cannot go to sea as a skipper without knowing the fundamentals like this. Operating on the assumption that just keeping out of the way is best is not good enough. It is irresponsible! Equally, a true understanding of weather, rigging, engines, communications, anchoring, and safety will keep you out of serious trouble. Having the skills to navigate away from and around rocks and dangerous objects is in the best interests of the lives of you and your family and friends. This is all theory. The practice is seeing it in action and experiencing it—holding a steady course, adjusting to the wind, and so much more. Thus, both theory and practice are important.

Upon completion of this course, you will be ready and fully prepared to experience practical training at any sailing training school worldwide or simply get out

Crossing situation.

on your own and try out what you have learned here. We also recommend that you gain lots of experience through friends with boats and at your local yacht club. We wrote an excellent blog on the topic of how to gain practical experience. You can read it by scanning the QR code to the right.

http://www.nauticed.org/sailing-blog/sailing-bucket-list/

As part of your purchase, we give you a free electronic sailor's logbook. We recommend that you begin to fill this out. You'll soon learn that you must report your experience in a résumé form to Yacht Charter Companies. Our free résumé building system works by drawing from your logbook entries. We explain all this in the QR code just below.

Finally, you're probably already starting to realize the value of this book. This is not just a grab-off-the-shelf-and-go-read book; this book ties you into the world's best sailing training program should you decide to pursue any further knowledge and certification. You're starting in exactly the right place. If you would like the understanding you have gained from reading this book added to your sailing résumé, you simply take the

test online at NauticEd.org. You will need to register for the Skipper Small Keelboat course. To do this, scan the QR code here. You'll then be taken to a website where you will get $18 off the price of the online course and test.

Now, let's get on with learning to be a great sailor, shall we?

To start, let us get you "in the mood" for a fun interactive sailing course. The boat featured in the short video to the right is a Beneteau First 20.

Chapter 1

Weather and Sea Conditions

The Joys of Sailing

A Beneteau First 25 under sail.

Sailing is ridiculously enjoyable! But a serious accident, injury, or loss of life is just not worth it. For the most part, these are all totally avoidable with knowledge, responsibility, and experience. So, you are to be commended for taking this course AND for taking it seriously. This is not something to power through and knock out for the sake of it or for the piece of paper certificate. There is information through-out this course that will save lives—yours or a family member's.

Since both weather and sea conditions are major influences in sailing, it is important that we begin the Skipper Small Keelboat course with these essentials.

The biggest killer in boating is weather, so you are well advised to take this chapter seriously, to continuously learn about weather and to be able to identify when it is safe to "enjoy boating" and when it is not safe.

In adverse weather conditions, safe boating is proportional to the size of your vessel. A smaller vessel will get tossed around more and is less able to handle wind and waves. There is also less protection from exposure to the weather.

As you gain experience, you'll begin to be more confident with a rough day out, and a good thrashing around can even become quite enjoyable. But always keep in mind your crew. The best way to scare off spouse, family member, kid, or friend from sailing forever is to have them screaming on the side rail, "TAKE ME HOME." It's much more prudent to introduce people to sailing on a nice day—sunny with 10 knots of breeze is perfect.

If you're an old-timer, remember the TV series *Hill Street Blues*? The sergeant always said to his team, "And Hey! Be careful out there."

Same here. Hey you with the boat, the weather can be a killer. Let's be careful out there. Check the weather and sail to your own confident ability!

Waves, Swell, and Depth

Since it is a good idea to keep your boat on top of the water, it's good to understand the dynamics of water.

Waves

Waves are the product of wind blowing across water.

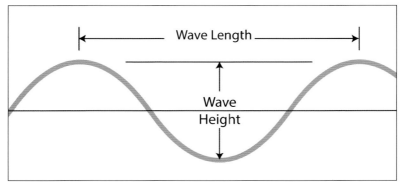

Wave metrics.

Wave height and wavelength metrics are shown at the bottom of the previous page. Another important metric is the Period. The Period of a wave is deemed as the time it takes for two consecutive crests to pass a stationary point. The frequency, although not used much in ocean wave metrics, is the number of waves to pass a stationary point in a certain amount of time (e.g., 10 waves per minute is a measure of the frequency, whereas the Period then would be stated as 1 wave per 6 seconds).

Since waves are primarily the result of surface wind action, they can be accurately predicted. Waves have troughs and crests. Sailing in moderate seas is safe and easy, but as waves grow, their capacity for doing harm is greatly increased and requires expert sailing skills.

As waves get steeper and steeper, the tops become tenably unstable. When propelled further by wind, the tops fall off, creating breaking waves. Take away the wind, and the tops return to being stable, but the waves themselves continue because there is nothing to stop them. This resultant wave is known as swell.

Swells

Swells are the result of waves from distant storms, sometimes thousands of miles away. Their wavelength is long, and they are generally not a problem, with one exception: many sailors are subject to seasickness because of swells.

Depth

Sailors need to be a little more cautious than recreational powerboaters. To prevent being pushed sideways through the water by the wind, sailboats have a big long thingy sticking down from the bottom of the boat. It's called a keel. For a smallish keelboat 22 ft (6.7 m) or so, the depth of the keel will be around 3-4 ft (1–1.3 m). The "rudder," which is the steering board thingy at the back, will be slightly shorter than the keel.

Modern, reliable **depth sounders** are electronic instruments that determine the distance from the keel to the sea floor by using ultrasound pulses. These devices can be set to

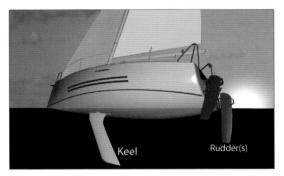

Keel versus water depth.

alert sailors when sailing close to shore, near atolls, or over other objects where you are uncertain about the water's depth. Fishfinders can be incorporated with them, allowing sailors to also check for fish activity, should you wish to catch the "big one."

Keep in mind that when sailing over areas that may have highly irregular bottom surfaces, such as coral, large rocks, and sunken objects, you may not have ample time to react to your depth sounder's warnings.

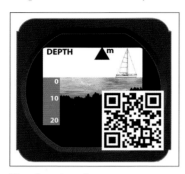

Depth animation.

Harbors are notorious for having fluctuating depths due to currents and poorly scheduled dredging. Be wary of water depth anytime you sail into a new harbor.

In the olden days, they used marked lines attached to lead weights to determine depth. Nowadays, we use sonar signals traveling at the speed of sound to measure the depth (and to determine if there are fish around for dinner). Still, a prudent sailor will have on board a backup lead weighted line. Recreationally speaking, it's not practical to have a bowman calling out the depth of water every minute. Thus, almost every vessel these days has a modern-day sonar depth finder. Every experienced sailor will tell you that the cost of a depth finder is worth the investment. If your vessel does not have one, get one.

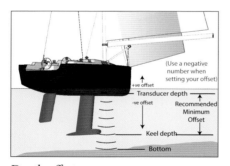

Depth offset.

Offset

Depth sounders have a feature that allows the depth reading to account for the depth of the keel. For example, if your keel is 5 feet deep and the real water depth is 20 feet, you will only have 15 feet of clearance. Thus, you want the depth reading to show 15 feet. Caution, however: when you set up your device, the offset number you need to put in is a negative number.

Tides

Tides are the regular rise and fall of the ocean due to gravitational forces from the moon and the sun. Tides vary in height all over the planet from zero to 50 ft (15 m), but for each specific location they rise and fall a similar amount each cycle.

Be especially wary of tides when anchoring. Anchor at high tide, and you may find your boat resting on the bottom in a few hours. Anchor at low tide, and you might find your boat drifting away in a few hours because the amount of anchor rode (anchor line) you put out did not account for the extra depth.

Fortunately, charts are marked with the low tide depth. But this is not all you need to know, as you'll discover later.

Boat at anchor.

A Rough Ride

Sailing becomes less than idyllic as sea state conditions worsen. While waves and swell are due to wind, there are some effects that can make them worse:

- Current—when current meets waves in differing directions, they create a confused heightened state of waves. Often, the waves become choppy and the wave length is decreased.
- When swells meet waves—superposition of these two can vastly increase the height and confusion of the sea.
- Distance from shore—when you have an offshore breeze, the waves get larger in height the farther from shore.
- Depth of water—as water gets shallower, wave height increases while also becoming steeper.

Understanding Weather Systems

Weather is a highly complex natural phenomenon. Globally, it is all connected and operates on a multitude set of physical laws. Consider these few that constantly bewilder and wonder us:

- heat travels through space from our very own star at the speed of light
- warm air rises while cold air sinks
- air wants to flow from high pressure to low pressure
- pressure decreases with altitude
- warm water releases vapor faster than cold water
- warm air holds more moisture than cold air
- the Coriolis effect turns wind right in front of our eyes
- the tilt of the earth creates the seasons

Predicting weather is one of humankind's most challenging tasks because of the many variables. It is indeed fickle stuff; it can be almost motionless one moment, and the next, it can move rapidly with tremendous speed and force. While there is not an app yet to control the weather, the good news is that there are now many

A hurricane over the Southeast U.S.

good sources to predict the weather, including apps on your smartphone and mobile devices.

Meteorology is the science of weather, and while forecasting weather is not yet an exact science, it is getting mighty good. Before going sailing, be sure to obtain the very latest weather conditions for your local area and prediction for the period you will be sailing.

Weather Sources

Global weather in general comes from unequal heating of masses of air at the earth's surface in places called "source regions." The main source regions are the snow-covered Arctic and Antarctic plains and tropical and subtropical oceans. Thus, an air mass might be cold and dry, cold and moist, warm and dry, or warm and moist. As the air moves, the planet rotates underneath it. This causes the rotation that we see on weather maps every day.

Air masses at different latitudes move around the planet in different directions. This is because at the equator, air is generally ascending. As surface air moves in to replace the ascending air, it turns west. At the polar regions, the air is generally descending. As air at the surface is pushed away from the polar regions, it turns east. Due to other more complicated effects, i.e., rotation and tilt, air from the equator descends back to the surface at about 30 degrees north and south latitudes. At 60 degrees north and south latitudes, air rises to descend again at the polar regions. This is called the three-cell model of general circulation.

It's not necessary to remember all this detail, but only to say that all these forces and movements create general trade winds, which sailors have been using for thousands of years. It's why cruisers go around the world in a counterclockwise direction, sticking to more equatorial latitudes with easterly winds and racers go around the

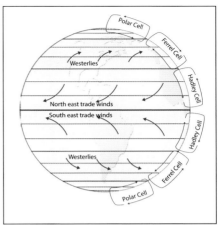

A three-cell model of general circulation.

world in a clockwise direction going as far south as possible with westerly winds. These forces and movements also create clashes of spinning air masses. It is these clashes that affect local conditions, creating cold and warm fronts and pressure gradients.

When a cold low-pressure mass of air clashes with a warmer mass of moist air, things are going to happen like frontal systems, which will be discussed soon.

Pressure

Air pressure is essentially the weight of all the air above pressing down. It is dependent on the density of the air and the temperature of the air in the exact column above. On a weather map, you see lots of circular and curved lines. These are isobars—lines of similar pressure. They are akin to gradient lines of height you see on a contour map showing mountains.

High-pressure areas are normally caused by a phenomenon called subsidence, meaning that as the air in the high cools, it becomes denser and moves toward the ground. Pressure increases here because more air fills the space left from the low. Subsidence also evaporates most of the atmosphere's water vapor so high-pressure systems are usually associated with clear skies and calm weather.

A high-pressure system, or "high," is an area where the atmospheric pressure is greater than that of the surrounding area. In some places, highs are referred to as anticyclones. These move clockwise in the northern hemisphere and counterclockwise in the southern due to the Coriolis effect.

A low-pressure system, or "low," is an area where the atmospheric pressure is lower than that of the surrounding area. Lows are usually associated with high

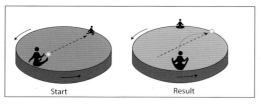

The Coriolis effect.

winds, warming air, and thus, the atmospheric lifting. Because of this, lows normally produce clouds, precipitation, and other bad weather such as tropical storms and cyclones.

Since low-pressure systems are referred to as cyclones, high-pressure systems are thus referred to as anticyclones.

As one might expect, wind likes to flow from high pressure to low pressure. But notice the words "like to." What actually happens is that while wind is moving, the earth is also turning, creating an effect on the wind called the Coriolis effect. This changes the wind's flow direction and results in a large circular motion about the pressure center. High-pressure systems spin one way and low-pressure systems spin the other, depending on whether they are situated in the northern or southern hemisphere.

As you get closer and closer to the center of a low, the pressure is dropping. This can be measured by a barometer. The lower the pressure, the more the wind has a propensity to move to the center of the low, which means higher wind speed. If you see the pressure dropping below 1000 mbar (millibars), then a low is approaching. Pressure in hurricanes gets down to about 900 mbar. Anything around 980 mbar will begin to feel uncomfortable for you in terms of higher winds.

Coriolis

The Coriolis effect is a fictional force that appears real in spinning objects like our planet earth. In the diagram at the top of the page, the first man rolls a ball to his

The Coriolis effect.

friend. But by the time the ball makes the distance, the friend has moved. To both, it appears as though the ball were acted upon by a constant turning force to make it veer off the original straight path. But there was no such force—it's just an effect that we observe.

Due to the Coriolis effect, in the northern hemisphere, the spin of the earth makes any air flowing **south** turn west, while in the southern hemisphere, the spin of the earth makes any air flowing **north** turn west. This is observed by areas of low pressure in the northern hemisphere turning counterclockwise, while areas of low pressure in the southern hemisphere turn clockwise. Essentially then, the winds follow the pressure lines angling in about 15 degrees in low-pressure zones and angling slightly outwards in high-pressure zones.

The easiest way to remember the spin directions is by the saying: "An anti-cyclone spins anticlockwise in the antipodes." (Australia and New Zealand were referred to as the antipodes in the olden days because they were directly opposite inhabitants of the northern hemisphere.)

Humidity and Moisture

Air holds water vapor in suspension. The amount of water it can hold depends on the temperature of the air and the pressure. For example, when the pressure is lowered by air rising, the air cannot hold as much water vapor, and thus the water comes out of suspension, resulting in clouds and rain. In lows, air is rising, and thus pressure is decreasing, resulting in clouds. In highs, air is descending and thus increasing in pressure. Moisture is absorbed into the air, resulting in clear sunny days.

Fronts

Fronts are completely different from lows and highs. The term "front" was coined when the phenomenon was understood and documented during the time of World War I. In a war, when two armies clashed, a front line was established. It was then similarly named when describing the clashing of two opposing air masses. It is important to understand these, as they generate significant changes in weather—sometimes fast. By seeing these on a weather map prior to heading out, you will be able to understand what is about to come.

Cold Front

A moving cold mass of air clashing into a stationary warm mass of air creates a "cold front." As the cold air strikes the warm, the warm air is immediately and violently lifted. As the warm air rises, water vapor is released. At the front line you will see massive clouds and rain and a sudden change in temperature. Isobar lines will also make a directional change due to a sudden change in pressure, affecting the wind direction. On the other side of the front, air is descending again, and thus you can have good clear visibility after the passing of the front.

On a weather map, a cold front is represented at the top of the next page.

Backing and Veering Winds

A wind direction changing to come from a more counter clockwise direction than it is now is called a backing wind. A veering wind is a wind changing to a more clockwise direction. For example, say you are in the northern hemisphere and looking north. The wind is coming from the southwest (7:30 o'clock to you). A cold front passes and the winds have changed to the northwest (10:30 o'clock to you). The winds thus changed clockwise (veering). This is typical in northern hemisphere cold front passages.

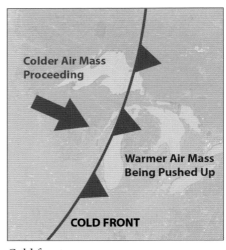

Cold front.

In southern hemisphere cold front passages, a typical wind change will be from northwest to southwest (backing).

A cross-sectional view of a cold front in the northern hemisphere is pictured below. Notice the drop in temperature and change in wind to a more clockwise direction.

Cloud definitions are:

- Ci = Cirrus
- Cs = Cirrostratus
- Cb = Cumulonimbus
- Ac = Altocumulus
- Cu = Cumulus

Warm Front

A moving mass of warm air clashing into a colder mass of air will spawn a warm front and is represented on the weather map at the top of the next page.

Cold front cross-section.

A cross-sectional view of a warm front in the northern hemisphere is pictured below the weather map on the next page. Notice the increase in temperature and change in the wind to a more counter-clockwise direction. The wind is a backing wind.

As the warm front approaches, clouds will become lower, and lower and barometric pressure will decrease because of the rising air. At the frontal boundary, ground fog can be formed due to the temperature change. The worst visibility condition with a warm front will occur as it passes, and immediately afterward, because of the moisture and possible rain in the air.

Occluded Front

Occluded fronts are linked with areas of low pressure called depressions (more on these soon!). When a depression forms, there is usually a warm front and a faster-moving cold front. The (northern hemisphere) diagram to the right, top, shows this. To the north of the warm front is the cool air that was in the area before the depression developed. When a cold front catches up to a warm front, the result is called an occluded front. A wide variety of weather can be found along an occluded front, with thunderstorms possible, but usually the occluded front passage is associated with a drying of the air mass. Occluded fronts can generate quite stormy weather as they pass over.

In the diagram to the right, the traveling warm air mass is replacing cooler air. At its leading edge is a warm front.

As the depression intensifies, the cold front catches up with the warm front (remember, a cold front moves faster than a warm front). The line where the two fronts meet is called an occluded front.

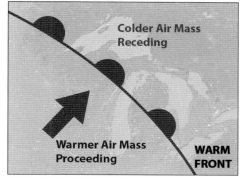

Warm front.

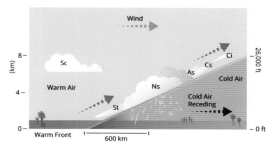

Warm front cross-section.

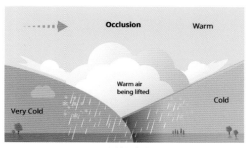

Occluded front cross-section.

Wind

Winds can be gentle, hardly felt, like zephyrs flitting about in a local area, or they can be vast movements of air moving swiftly across oceans and continents at low and high altitudes.

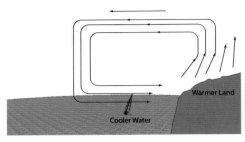

Sea breeze.

Sea breezes are a local area scale of the effect of differential heating of air. They are well known to experienced sailors.

In the diagram above and to the right, a parcel of air over land in summer at noon will be warmed more than a parcel over water. Both are receiving the same amount of solar heat, but it takes more heat to raise water one degree than it does for land. Hence, the parcel over the warmer land will rise, while the heavier, cooler air over the water will flow in under it to take its place.

This phenomenon gives birth to the so-called daytime "sea breeze."

The reverse occurs at night, particularly on clear nights when the earth can radiate a lot of heat out to space. Now, air warmed by the water rises and is replaced by the descending cooler air over the land, driving the air flow in the reverse direction and creating a "land breeze." This can surprise an unwary sailor, when as the night wears on and he sleeps at anchor, the land breeze alters the wind and his boat swings to a new direction. Did he consider this effect when he anchored?

During daytime hours, sea breezes can yield useful sailing conditions just next to a coast, when there might be no wind farther offshore and none otherwise shown in weather forecasts.

Light surface winds produce "cat paw"-looking waves, whereas stronger winds produce sharper and higher waves. As winds increase, energy is transferred to the water, waves become higher, and spray begins blowing off the crests of waves. Experienced sailors can often accurately determine wind speed by watching the wave.

When reading a weather map or wind map, you need to know the symbols used. Make sure you understand this table, especially the direction. The circles are the heads of the arrow, whereas the barbs are their tails.

SYMBOLS EXPLAINED		
Symbol	Wind Direction	Wind Speed
○	Indeterminate Direction	Zero
		1 short barb = 5 knots
		1 long barb = 10 knots
		1 short 2 long = 25 knots
		1 penant = 50 knots

In compass-named directions, the wind directions in the table on page 12 are:

- 5 knots northeasterly
- 10 knots northwesterly
- 25 knots easterly
- 50 knots south-southeasterly

The following table is a rough summary of wind speed and its effect. The column on reefing is of course a matter of choice and boat type. For example, in the large catamarans, you'll reef the mainsail first because of its larger size over the genoa. Roller furling systems allow the crew to reef the sails to any position. However, the sails will typically have marks on them for the recommended first reef and second reef points. Expected boat speed is stated for an average cruising type boat. Race boats can go much faster.

Wind Speed (knots)	Wave Action	Expected Boat Speed (knots)	Effect on Boat and Reefing Recommendation
0–5	calm-ripples	0–2 knots	No heeling
6–10	1–2ft (0.3–0.6 m)	2–6 knots	Slight heeling
11–15	2–4ft (0.6–1.3 m) white caps	6–10 knots	Moderate to heavy heeling
16–25	4–8ft (1.3–2.6 m)	6–12 knots	Reefing required heavy heeling
25–35	6–15 ft (2–4.6 m) spray	6–12 knots	2nd reef required—danger, return to base ASAP—seek shelter
35+	8–20 ft (2.6–6.3 m)	6–12 knots	Max reefing–extreme danger, seek immediate shelter. Employ storm tactics.

Another scale: The Beaufort Wind Scale is both historically and visually very interesting. It was designed by a British Francis Admiral (Admiral Beaufort) to help large, fully rigged vessels determine their sail requirements. It is a classic and still useful for today's sailors as a guide and component of your dreams to be a frigate captain.

THE BEAUFORT WIND SCALE

Force	Wind (Knots)	WMO Classification	Appearance of Wind Effects On the Water
0	Less than 1	Calm	Sea surface smooth and mirror-like
1	1–3	Light Air	Scaly ripples, no foam crests
2	4–6	Light Breeze	Small wavelets, crests glassy, no breaking

3	7–10	Gentle Breeze	Large wavelets, crests begin to break, scattered whitecaps
4	11–16	Moderate Breeze	Small waves 1–4 ft. becoming longer, numerous whitecaps
5	17–21	Fresh Breeze	Moderate waves 4–8 ft taking longer form, many whitecaps, some spray
6	22–27	Strong Wind Warning	Larger waves 8–13 ft, whitecaps common, more spray
7	28–33	Near Gale	Sea heaps up, waves 13–20 ft, white foam streaks off breakers
8	34–40	Gale	Moderately high (13–20 ft) waves of greater length, edges of crests begin to break into spindrift, foam blown in streaks
9	41–47	Strong Gale	High waves (20 ft), sea begins to roll, dense streaks of foam, spray may reduce visibility
10	48–55	Storm	Very high waves (20–30 ft) with overhanging crests, sea white with densely blown foam, heavy rolling, lowered visibility
11	56–63	Violent Storm	Exceptionally high (30–45 ft) waves, foam patches cover sea, visibility more reduced
12	64+	Hurricane	Air filled with foam, waves over 45 ft, sea completely white with driving spray, visibility greatly reduced

This is pretty hard to remember. Thus, look at the table on page 13 and above and remember the wind conditions force number that you are comfortable sailing in. If force conditions are reported worse, then you know not to go out or prepare if you are already out. Generally speaking, force 4 is 11-to-16 knots. This is comfortable for most.

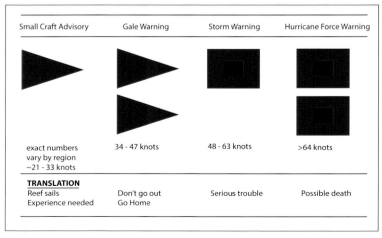

Wind warning flags.

Yacht clubs and some harbormasters may fly flags to indicate any wind warnings. These are not internationally standardized, so it is best you check for your country and state (yes, even states are different in the USA). Don't go sailing in anything above Small Craft Advisory, and note that a Small Craft Advisory is a warning to those in small craft that conditions are dangerous. If you are inexperienced, you should not go out under small craft advisory conditions.

On the bottom of the previous page is a table of the most common wind warning flags. They are more commonly used in the USA, but some other countries also use them.

Gusts

Gusts can occur at virtually anytime and can be extremely dangerous for several reasons.

- If not properly handled, a gust can overpower the rig and cause the mast to come down (demasting).
- A gust heels the boat over and throws the crew and gear around.
- A gust heels the boat making the rudder less effective and thus rounds the boat up into wind and into crossing traffic, causing a collision.
- A gust can broach the boat when sailing with a spinnaker. A broach is like a round up into wind except the boat is held down and on its side because of the spinnaker. It can cause sinking.
- A gust can cause the boom to gybe over unexpectedly, killing crew members who have their heads up.

Gusts can be seen coming by a moving discoloration of the water. Good crew members point out approaching gusts to the helmsperson and prepare for action such as letting out the mainsail traveler or mainsheet. Helmspersons can prepare to adjust course.

Right, top, is a series of gusts in "The Bight" in Norman Island, British Virgin Islands.

Right, bottom, is a series of gusts created by Katabatic winds in the Marlborough Sounds, New Zealand.

In General

Always keep in mind that you never want to overpower your vessel, as this can lead to catastrophic results. As wind velocities increase, the force on a sailboat's rigging and sails is dramatically increased by the squared power. As examples: if the wind speed doubles from 5 knots to 10 knots, the force on the rigging quadruples; from 5 knots to 20 knots, the force becomes 16 times greater.

Clouds, Fog, Thunderstorms

Clouds

Clouds can give a relatively easy and quick look at what might be coming in the future. Compare these in the two cross-sections of warm and cold fronts presented earlier. Notice that both warm and cold fronts are preceded by Cirrus clouds. These clouds, then, are a good indication of possible changing weather in the next few days.

But, because there is so much going on in the atmosphere, any serious prediction of weather from cloud observations is difficult unless you are a complete expert. Given that most of us are not expert meteorologists, it is better to heed to the information on your smartphone.

Below are the most common clouds.

Cirrus Clouds: very high and wispy. Possible warm or cold front approaching.

Altocumulus Clouds: very high, small, and cotton ball shape.

Cumulus Clouds: cotton ball shape. Fair weather clouds. Not too much happening.

Cumulonimbus Clouds: tall puffy clouds often associated with severe thunderstorms. Watch out for these.

Fog

Since fog is one of the more menacing weather conditions that may occur because of the risk of collision, it is prudent to obtain knowledge about the possibility before leaving the slip or anchorage. Fog banks can often be observed as they move into an area. Whenever fog occurs, the vessel must have a plan of action. These include:

- knowing and making the proper sound signals
- posting crew specifically to maintain lookout
- using radar and AIS if available
- maintaining slow speed

- using your VHF to contact other vessels and inquire about conditions around you

Fog enveloping the Golden Gate Bridge.

Fog may occur as a relatively local event, often near shore, by rolling off the land, or it may cover a huge geographical area. Fog occurs when the air becomes saturated with moisture by a changing temperature and/or air pressure condition. Over land, radiation fog occurs when the land cools and subsequently, the air next to it cools and moisture drops out, forming fog. Remember that colder air holds less moisture.

Advection fog over the water can be generated by warm, moist air blowing over a cold sea, just like your breath on a cold morning. And unlike land-based morning fog, advection fog doesn't necessarily mean it will burn off as the day warms up.

The many conditions that may lead to fog formation make it prudent for sailors to know what these are for your local area. However, professional forecasting is now very good and should be monitored.

Electric Thunderstorms

Electric storms are frightening. On inland waters, they can arrive very quickly, especially on a hot, sultry day. Electric storms are frequently accompanied by high and very erratic winds. Huge wind bullets, which are sudden wind gusts, can come seemingly out of nowhere.

While you should always be prepared for a storm, when you observe a heavy cloud formation rising rapidly with huge white clouds, called "thunderheads," it is time to make further preparations. Get to a safe harbor if time permits. If not, prepare for a storm: reef the mainsail, lower the jib sail, douse spinnakers, close hatches, keep away from metal objects if possible, put on life jackets, turn off electronic gear. Crew safety is paramount.

If a violent thunderstorm is approaching, take all sails down and turn on engines. Reduce the apparent wind velocity on your boat by running downwind.

Scan the code to the right and view this awesome microburst video, which shows a thunderstorm producing deadly winds.

If you sail in a thunderstorm-prone area, you should consider seeking professional help in the installation of lightning protection gear for your vessel.

Lightning occasionally strikes vessels on lakes or on the open ocean. Lightning rods on top of masts and connected to metallic pathways to the ocean can help prevent damage to a sailboat.

When encountering an electric storm, it's best to leave the area and get off the water. If this is not possible, then get everyone below decks. Do not touch metal objects. While theoretically, your mast is insulated from the water in most

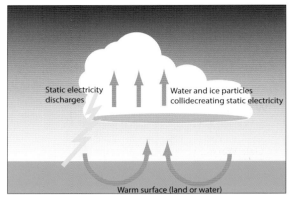

Static electricity.

vessels, at the voltage levels generated in lightning, the electrical discharge can jump across the insulating materials. Much of this can be avoided by checking the weather before you go out to see if there is storming activity.

There is an old myth that says to wrap your anchor chain around the mast and put it into the water to allow lightning to travel overboard and not into the boat. This is certainly a myth, and every lightning engineer will tell you that lightning will not travel around the right angle turn from the mast to the chain.

Weather Predictions

Before modern-day digital forecasting and its cool electronic toys like doppler radar and satellite imaging, sailors feared the weather on every outing, and rightly so. Bad weather and death were potentially always just around the corner. Today, the cool toys tell us just about everything. But that means that the modern-day sailor must use and understand how to use the cool toys. There is no room on earth for the lackadaisical recreational sailor who goes out on the water without checking the forecast.

Philosophers have repeatedly said: we all talk about the weather, but there are very few things we can do about it. While this is still true today, we have real-time knowledge about approaching weather conditions, thus allowing us to be better prepared. Gone are the days when a hurricane will hit without warning. In September 1900, 8,000 people

were killed in Galveston, Texas, during a category 4 hurricane. They simply did not know it was coming, nor did they have time to get out of its way.

Today, information about weather conditions is updated in real-time and made available to every mariner. Even at sea, mariners can get instant information via satellite. And even better, computer weather forecasting models are mature, and predictions are accurate. Everybody has their own favorite personal weather anecdote, based on aching joints or running noses, about what the weather will be like. These folk tales should not be taken too seriously, but weather forecasts should.

Weather Forecast Terms

Table of Terms Used in Forecasting	
Gale Warnings	Average wind is expected to be F8 or more or gusts 43-51 kn
Strong Wind Warnings	Average wind is expected to be F6-7. F6 is often called a yachtsman's gale
Imminent	Within 6 hours of the time of issuing the warning
Soon	Within 6-12 hrs of the time of issuing the warning
Later	More than 12 hours from the time of issuing the warning
Visibility	GOOD = greater than 5 miles (8km) MODERATE = between 2 to 5 miles (3.3 km to 8km) POOR = 0.6 miles to 2 miles (1km to 3.3km) FOG = less than 0.6 miles (1000m)
Fair	No significant precipitation
Backing	Wind changing in an anticlockwise (counterclockwise) direction. e.g. from NW to SW
Veering	Wind changing in a clockwise direction. e.g. from NE to SE
General Synopsis	How and where the weather systems are moving
Sea States	Wave heights: SMOOTH = 8 in. to 20 in. (0.2 - 0.5 m) SLIGHT = 8 in. to 4 ft (0.5 - 1.25 m) MODERATE = 4 ft to 8 ft (1.25 - 2.5 m) ROUGH = 8 ft to 13 ft (2.5 - 4 m) VERY ROUGH = 13 ft to 20 ft (4 - 6 m)

Weather Information

Nowadays, sources of weather information are virtually limitless. There is no excuse, and it is an amateurish mistake, to be caught out unawares by weather because you did not bother to look. Yes, you might be miles out to sea when a weather system develops or a tropical depression turns in your direction, but you will know it is coming and you can form a tactic to outrun it prior to its arrival. Cook, Drake. and Magellan had no such luxury.

Here are the major sources of weather information:

- VHF radio, fixed mounted or handheld
- Online Internet access

- Weather fax
- Television and radio stations
- Streaming audio from a list of USA and Canadian sites (see QR code)
- Smart phone and Device Apps
- Subscription services for serious sailors wanting accuracy

VHF Radio

Tuning into one of the 1 to 9 VHF weather channels designated for your area will provide a local forecast as well as for close surrounding areas. This information is updated and repeated continually, 24 hours a day. A quick search on the Internet will give the VHF channel for your local area.

The Internet

Weather information is constantly gathered, updated, and disseminated by a vast number of websites. A quick search will render ones to your liking. Here are some common USA and global ones:

NOAA (National Oceanic Atmospheric Administration)		Wind Guru	
NWS (National Weather Service)		The Weather Channel	
Weather Underground		Predict Wind (subscription— highly accurate data)	

Apps

PocketGrib

One of our favorite apps for weather information is called Pocket GRIB. This clever app downloads on demand an extremely small **GRI**dded **B**inary file and overlays into the software in the app. You can select anywhere in the world for which you

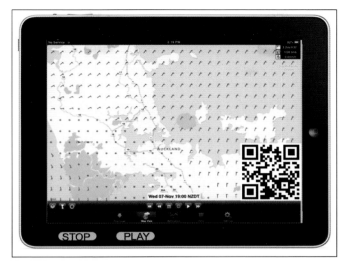

Pocket GRIB animation.

want the information, and you get a forecast up to 5 days. The reason it is so cool is that the data packet is extremely small, which saves on cell data rates if you are in a place where you're using roaming data.

Tap the image for an animation. This opens under a new tab—just close it when finished with the observations. Notice that as the animation plays, the conditions change with date and time. It ends with a tabular view of the same. Watch it a few times.

PocketGRIB for iPhone   PocketGRIB for Android

PocketGRIB for iPad

WunderGround

Besides being a good website, the WunderGround app—WunderMaps—is also pretty good. It uses the Internet directly to present information.

WunderMaps by Weather Underground—for iPhone and iPad

WunderMaps by Weather Underground—for Android

Below is a screen shot of the WunderMaps app showing frontal systems.

WunderMaps app.

PredictWind

PredictWind is also a web AND app source of information. Some of it is free and some is a paid subscription.

PredictWind—for iPhone and iPad

Predict-Wind—for Android

Other Apps

With apps getting added seemingly every day, we're supplying this widget to search for apps on the iTunes store.

Subscription Services

Subscription services are by far the best source of information, and most have a semilimited free version for which you can sign up. Or, for 20 bucks a year, you can get amazing detail—sometimes down to 1km resolution. Plus, they have packages specially designed for sailors, including forecast tables and graphs, wind maps, swell maps, rain maps, cloud maps, isobar maps, sea temperature maps, GBIB files, weather routing, tides, currents, departure planning, GPS tracking, forecast alerts, realtime observations. And all this information is in one place! If you're serious about sailing, you should be subscribing to one of these services. At the very least, have a poke around these companies listed below to see what they offer. Plus, if you're into racing, this is going to give you a huge advantage.

PredictWind

This is a web-based subscription service. You get all the information via the web down to 1km resolution. Below is an example of winds off the coast of New Zealand for a specific day. Colors represent wind strengths—or you can view by a data table. Predict wind also has apps for iPhone, iPad, and Android.

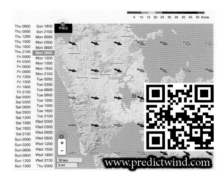

PredictWind map.

ClearPoint Weather

With ClearPoint Weather, you first download the number-crunching software onto your computer. The software then pulls in raw data from the Internet each time you want updated conditions or an updated weather prediction for a specific area. This type of service can allow you to get incredibly accurate conditions and predictions. The advantage here is that only small amounts of data are coming in for each prediction. If you're racing, or doing a crossing or any multiday coastal navigation, this is the serious power that you need. The package also includes weather routing for fastest times or storm avoidance. Considering the nature of weather, a small investment like this is worth it.

Observing a Weather Map

By learning to read a weather map, you can gain a lot of knowledge about coming weather conditions.

Here is a typical situation in the northern hemisphere:

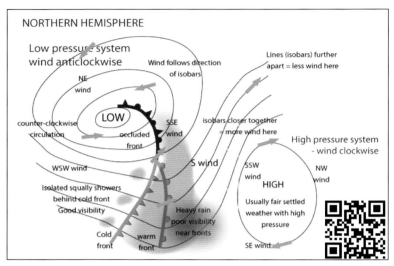

Northern hemisphere weather systems.

And here is a typical situation in the southern hemisphere:

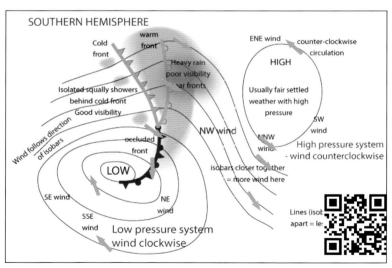

Southern hemisphere weather systems.

The bottom line is that the weather we sail in is seldom stable, forecasts are becoming more predictable, but sailors need to use the technology and also be constantly alert to changes.

Weather Warnings

Weather services will also provide **weather warnings**, such as small craft or gale warnings for a certain area, as well as fog predictions. These warnings are very accurate and should be heeded. Small craft advisory and gale warning pennants (flags) may be flown in some marinas and other official locations alerting day sailors to be wary of conditions as they leave a sheltered harbor.

For any country and/or local area, it is a good idea now to search around for your local warnings issued via web interface.

For the USA, you can use the National Weather Service.

Or for any country including the USA, wunderground.com is a good reference to search for severe weather warnings.

Major storms also get major media coverage. However, just because you know a storm is coming, you must also know how to get out of its path in adequate time. Heavy weather should be avoided at all costs by inexperienced sailors, regardless of how strong the vessel may be.

Today there is little excuse for sailors not knowing quite specifically what kind of weather they will encounter if they simply use the weather services freely available on board a vessel, such as handheld VHF radios or apps.

In summary, before beginning any sailing adventure, be it a short day sail or an extended journey, check the weather and sea conditions at your destination and monitor your weather throughout the voyage.

Heavy rainstorm in Anegada, BVI.

If you have major trepidations about weather or sea, the prudent thing is to stay in your slip until you are convinced your sailing skills are capable of handling the existing weather and sea conditions.

Clothing

New Zealander Sir Edmund Hillary and Nepalese Tenzing Norgay were the first to summit Mt. Everest in 1953. Compared to today, clothing technology had not even been invented. In 1958, Sir Edmund went on to the South Pole traveling there in a Ferguson farm tractor. Can you imagine a wool jumper, nylon jacket, and leather boots with wool socks?

Wet and cold is not your friend. Nowadays, clothing technology is amazing and will do the job of warm and dry. There are many companies producing very high quality sailing gear in which you should invest. Gill, Helly Hansen, Henri Floyd, Musto are a few to name. And compared again to the 1950s, some of it can look quite stylish—even for the ladies.

Scan the code at right for a good description of layering. Tap on each layer.

If you own a boat, here's a tip: Take a bag, put a complete change of clothing of various sizes in the bag, zip it up, and stow it on the boat. Then every season, take out the bag and wash all the clothing to get rid of any musty smell. Why? Man overboard! That's why. Last time we had a man overboard, I was very impressed with the owner. Out came the bag and back into the race we went with a very grateful crew member.

Also, keep on board a bottle of sunscreen, spare sunglasses, a few different size jackets hanging up in a closet, spare hats, and a blanket including a hypothermia blanket. As a captain, you are responsible for the crew at all times. This includes being prepared for the unprepared crew member.

Dressing appropriately for weather conditions is an important topic that is often overlooked. Weather in the slip may be considerably different from weather over a body of water. In general, it will be cooler on the water, but the sun can be brutal as rays reflect off the water. Choices include slathering on sunscreen, donning rain-repellent slickers, and of course looking "sailorish." Marine stores have caught on to these needs and now offer many suggestions and products.

Chapter 2

Electrical and Mechanical

Introduction

One day you will be stuck out there. There will be no wind and it will be getting dark. You'll need to rely on and have the knowledge of the electrical and mechanical systems on your boat. You simply cannot afford a failure of either one.

Electrical systems drive, most important, your vessel lights so that you can be seen. Other boats are relying on your lights and the proper colors of your lights to identify you and the direction you are heading. You must understand batteries, circuit breakers, wiring, and charging systems. Being run down by a high-speed ferry in the middle of the night is quite undesirable.

Also important is the automatic bilge pump that is driven by electricity. Splashing down into 6 inches of water in the main cabin is not a good feeling; neither is arriving at the dock, planning to go sailing, only to see your mast poking out of the water due to a simple failure of the bilge pump.

The major mechanical system on a small boat is your outboard engine. Having to sail in through the breakwater is not a good option; neither is sailing up to the dock or mooring ball under gale or zero-wind conditions.

Batteries

The electrical system on a small sailboat is entirely driven by Direct Current (DC) electricity. The major onboard source of DC electricity is one, or sometimes 2, 12-volt batteries. These batteries are similar to automobile batteries, except that the batteries best suited for a small boat are called deep cycle batteries and are specifically designed for low energy (low amperage) drain rate, whereas car batteries are designed for high energy (high amperage) drain rate for engine cranking during starting.

These powerful DC batteries are classified into three major categories depending on the following characteristics:

Wet or flooded batteries that contain lead plates, fixed in a mixture of distilled water and sulfuric acid. These have been the most common for many years and must be serviced regularly.

Batteries containing a gel material instead of liquid, which allows them to be sealed, thus minimal service is required.

Absorbed glass mat (AGM) batteries that contain micro fiberglass. These represent the latest technology and are best suited for the marine environment. Although they are generally the most expensive, they are usually worth it in the long run.

Each of these categories of batteries has unique characteristics and differs widely in initial costs and ongoing maintenance. All tend to be heavy and are usually stored low in the vessel (generally under a settee near the vessel's center). They should be firmly secured and should receive proper care as prescribed.

We recommend staying with one category of battery and not mixing newer types and older types. What they all have in common is that they require regular inspection and attention when needed. Almost sounds like they have personalities.

On a small boat there is typically only one battery and thus no redundant supply. When the battery goes out, it is out. Murphy's Law says this will happen at the most inopportune time! In this case, it is especially wise to load test your battery each season. Load testing is more than just a voltmeter; a load tester is a device that causes a drain on the battery and measures the battery's response. You can get one at your local auto parts store, or just take your battery in for a test.

Sometimes, two batteries are often wired together in such a manner that they can be used separately or in pairs. If you wire two batteries together, you must do so "in parallel." This means Positive on one battery to Positive on the other battery and Negative to Negative. This keeps the output voltage at 12 volts. Wiring "in series" will result in 24 volts, which will blow up your circuits and bulbs and bilge pumps and . . .

If multiple batteries are installed, there is usually some sort of switch to operate them. In the event of an electrical fire, you should turn the battery switches to the off position as quickly as possible.

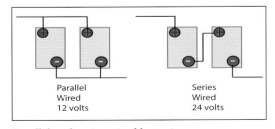

Parallel and series wired batteries.

Battery Charging

Keeping your batteries fully charged is done either by a small solar panel or an AC battery charger powered from the 110 volt (USA) or 240 volt (most of the rest of the world) AC shore supply.

Solar

Solar panels for charging your battery system are ideal because they are reliable, whereas dock shore supply is subject to the next guy in the slip not tripping out the power supply circuit breaker when they drop their cord in the water. Additionally, intermittent, faulty, sparking shore power connections are one of the major sources of fire to boats in marinas.

Solar panels are either hard or flexible and about 12 inches (.3 m) each side. They are available through any chandlery or online. Batteries like solar chargers because car/marine batteries always like to be fully charged—it makes them last longer.

AC Battery Chargers

An AC power line is run onto the boat from the shore power to charge the batteries. This is typically the only use for AC on a smaller boat.

The battery charger will probably be mounted under a settee.

The battery charger is typically hardwired to the DC circuit. Thus, you need to do nothing to charge the batteries except plug in the AC shore power to the boat upon your return to the dock.

There may be an AC electric panel next to the DC panel. It will have an "AC Main" On/Off switch and a Battery Charger On/Off switch.

The switch and/or breaker for this circuit is especially important, as it is the charger that keeps your 12-volt DC batteries fully charged. The standard procedure is to keep the charger activated at all times, even when hooked up to shore power. This will ensure that you will always have adequate 12-volt DC power.

Modern DC battery chargers are designed to not overcharge your batteries even when left on indefinitely.

Severe caution should be used to ensure the AC shore plug is tightly connected. This faulty connection is the biggest source of fire damage to boats.

AC Solar panels.

DC Panel

The DC panel seems intimidating at first, but each switch has a distinct function.

When you first enter the cabin, you will want to turn on all those that are necessary for your outing. Make a habit of keeping off those that are not needed.

Each switch also serves as a circuit breaker; so, in the event of an electric fire onboard, you will need to turn these off immediately.

The most frequently used light switches are typically the:

- Navigation Lights: Red (port), Green (starboard) and White (aft)
- Steaming Lights (used when operating under power at night)
- Anchor light (used when at anchor at night)
- Cabin lights
- Cockpit lights

DC electric panel.

Almost always you will turn on the instruments (depth, speed, and other mounted instruments) and if you feel like jamming out—the stereo.

The bilge pump is almost always set up to come on automatically should water rise above a certain level. The bilge switch is usually only a manual "on" and thus, the switch typically is just left in the off position.

Bilge Pump

This is a typical bilge pump:

It will either have a built-in float switch or one mounted right next to it in the lowest point of the boat under a floor panel.

The float switch is appropriately named. It floats up when the water level rises and then makes the electrical connection to automatically turn it on. It's a good idea to make the bilge pump part of your seasonal safety checkout.

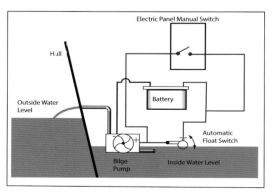

Bilge pump wiring.

For those interested, it is typically wired-in as in the diagram at the bottom of the previous page. Note that the automatic float switch system bypasses the electrical panel switch.

Battery Management

It's easy to run down the batteries when out all day and night having fun, blasting the stereo, and having the cabin lights and fans on. In boating life, you have to learn to be a conservationist: conserve electricity, fuel, and water. They are limited.

To reduce the consumption of electricity, light bulbs on a sailboat can be swapped out to be LED-type bulbs, which are far less of a power consumer.

Just be wary of your power consumption and make sure you've always got enough left for essential safety operations like navigation lights to get home.

Electrical Emergencies

Under no condition can you tolerate a fire on a vessel.

A few words of caution: batteries are designed to put out an enormous amount of current. An inadvertent short between two wires will cause excessive heat in the wires and can build up over a relatively short period, causing an electrical fire.

Electrical fire is the most common source of fire on boats. The immediate response to first smelling smoke or discovery of fire is to assume it is caused by an electrical source. In this case:

1. Sound the alarm.
2. Turn off the main battery switch. This entails knowing where it is as part of your initial boat familiarization tour on any new boat.
3. If flames occur, use an appropriate fire extinguisher rated for electrical fires. See Chapter 10 for the discussion on fire types and appropriate extinguishers.
4. Ascertain from which circuit the fire originated.
5. Turn off the circuit breaker to the faulty circuit.
6. Only after success with parts 3 and 4 above, if you need power back on, turn on the battery switch and carefully monitor the situation.

If the fire is not flaming, you may just allow a few moments for it to cool down. But only turn the main battery switch back on once the faulty circuit has been identified.

Never, ever, pour water on an electrical fire where electricity is still present. Water conducts electricity.

If you have turned off all devices, including your running lights at night, you will need to take precautions, like posting a lookout with a flashlight to alert other vessels.

Failing to have sufficient DC battery power can have wide-ranging implications including being unable to use running lights at night or the navigational instruments. For this reason, it is advisable to have as an essential safety item one each of white, green, and red portable back-up navigation lights.

Portable back-up lights are relatively inexpensive, and you can find them with a quick Google search. Or just visit your local chandlery, which more than likely will have them in stock. Some have suction mounts, some have C-clamps, and some mount on the pulpit railing. Obviously, they should be stowed in an easily accessible place—as reported by the near-miss ferry situation above—AND the batteries should be checked often.

Backup navigation lights.

Outboard Engine

The outboard engine is your friend but can be the biggest source of your frustrations. AND, if not managed properly, it can lead you into dangerous situations.

Parts of the Engine

Fuel and Oil

It's very important to know if your engine is 2-stroke or 4-stroke because of the fuel/oil mixture. Since boats tend to be used infrequently, it is a very good idea to condition your

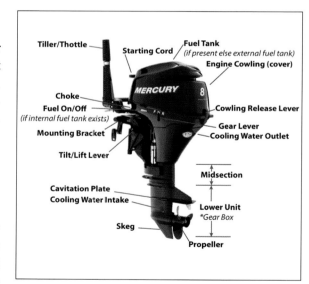

Parts of a typical outboard.

fuel to prevent buildup of deposits, gum, and varnish.

See this fuel condition brochure by Mercury at right.

At fueling stations globally, fuels go by different colloquial names:

- Diesel, gazole, and gasoil are synonymous
- Petrol, Petroleum, gas, and gasoline are synonymous

2-Stroke Engines

2-stroke engines require 2-stroke oil as well as gasoline. Sometimes these are mixed automatically by the engine, and sometimes you must mix them together yourself. Oil is mixed with the fuel in a 2-stroke engine because the oil is used as a lubricant during the combustion process. It is absolutely essential that you do not ignore the 2-stroke oil mix or levels; if you do, you will burn out the engine within minutes of operation. No lubrication leads to excessive heat from increased friction, which leads to engine death. Additionally, you cannot substitute 2-stroke oil for regular oil.

The typical mix ratios are 25 parts of fuel to 1 part of oil or 50 parts of fuel to 1 part oil, but you must consult the engine manual. It's also a good idea to put your own mix ratio label inside the cabin or fuel canister storage area. On board your boat you should have a measuring bottle that will list the amount of oil for the correct ratio for a specific amount of fuel.

You will know if the engine is 2-stroke because there will always be a giant sign on the engine saying "2 Stroke." If you are unsure, consult the manual or look up the model on the Internet.

Note that a 2-stroke oil/gas mix can "go off" usually after about four or so months. So it's a good idea to replace the mix if you have not used your boat in a while.

To summarize, for 2-stroke engines:

- Know if the fuel is mixed automatically by the engine or if you must mix it into the fuel tank yourself.
- Learn the mix ratio of fuel to oil.
- Only use 2-stroke oil.

4-Stroke Engines

4-stroke engines are more like car engines. They do not require 2-stroke oil. Be careful if you are bringing fuel from another engine to yours. The other engine might be 2-stroke

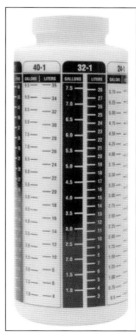

Fuel mix measuring bottle.

when yours is 4-stroke or vice versa. You will damage your engine if this is done in either case.

4-stroke engines have a sump of regular oil whereby a dipping arm from the crankshaft lifts oil to disperse over the inside of the engine to keep it lubricated. Thus, it is important to ensure this sump of oil is filled to its required level, just like a car.

To summarize, for 4-stroke engines:

- Never use a mix of 2-stroke oil.
- Only use normal engine oil for the sump (not 2-stroke oil).

The advantage of 4-stroke engines is that they run quieter, are more fuel efficient, and don't put out obnoxious exhaust fumes that can make your crew quickly become sick when motoring downwind. Fumes + wave action = puke!

The Fuel Tank and Hose

Your engine will either have an external fuel tank connected to the engine by a hose or a built-in fuel tank on the top of the engine; sometimes it will have both. The external tank typically holds about 5 gallons, or 20 liters. Both external tanks and built-in tanks will typically have a vent on the top. You must loosen the vent to allow air to get into the tank as the fuel is used; otherwise, this creates a vacuum inside the tank and eventually prevents the fuel from flowing out. The symptom of this is that the engine stops with fuel still remaining in the tank. The fix is to open the fuel vent. If there is a hose from the tank to the engine, you will need to squeeze the hose bulb (explained below) until it hardens full of fuel.

Fuel tank.

The fuel hose has two connectors, one for the tank and the other for the engine. It also has a squeeze bulb in between. The squeeze bulb is a manual hand pump that forces fuel to the engine. You usually give it a couple of squeezes before you start the engine. If the bulb is empty, you will be able to completely collapse the bulb; if so, continue squeezing until the bulb becomes filled with fuel (you will feel it harden). When you are replacing the tank after filling or if you have run the tank dry, the bulb will also need pumping to harden.

A note on refueling: it's a really bad idea to refuel the tanks from a larger tank on the boat. Spillage into our waterways is not an option. If you must, use a simple no-spill siphon hose which you can see by scanning the code to the right. You just wobble it up and down a bit, and the one-way valve starts the siphoning. Otherwise, do your refueling on land.

Built-in Fuel Tank

Some engines have a tank built into the top of the engine. If this is the case, there will be a fuel shutoff valve and probably a fuel primer pump button to prime the carburetor with a small amount of fuel prior to starting. The big mistake that everyone makes is forgetting to turn on the fuel valve. Many times the engine will start with the valve closed because of a residual amount of fuel in the line. The engine will quickly stop—usually within about 1 minute—at the most inopportune time.

The Choke

Usually, you pull out the choke, pull the starter cord 2-3 times, then push back in the choke back in. Otherwise, you will flood the engine.

Starting

It's a gorgeous day and you're eager to get the engine going and get out on the water. You pull the start cord and drive your elbow right into the face of your spouse. That is the end of sailing today. And the end of a few other things for a while, too!

Before each pull, check your elbow room!

Starting Procedure:

- Check fuel connections
- Check tank vents
- Turn on fuel lever on side of the engine (if it exists)
- If using an external tank, pump the hose bulb 2 times or until filled (It will feel hard when you squeeze it)
- Ensure the engine is out of gear
- Turn the throttle to its starting position
- Pull out the choke lever
- Check elbows (check again)
- Check elbows (check again)

- Pull the starter cord
- Brmmm brmmm
- Push in the choke lever

It should be as simple as that!

Often you will find that the engine is "flooded" and will not start. Flooded means there is too much fuel in the firing chamber compared to the oxygen available and the ignition is being prevented. The fix for this is simple: just turn the throttle all the way open. This allows more air into the chamber. Pull a few more times with the throttle all the way open, and you'll usually get a start. Quickly reduce the throttle after starting to prevent overly revving the engine.

After starting, allow the engine to warm a little before applying more throttle. This increases the life of the engine because revving the engine after a cold start creates a lot of friction and thus wear.

Before engaging the gear, make sure the throttle is set low and the engine is idling. Otherwise, you run the risk of stripping out the gearbox. And Murphy will make sure that happens right at the breakwater.

After starting, you must ensure that the water pump is working. This is usually easily seen by a thin stream of water being pumped out into the water under the casing of the engine. This is the cooling water for the engine. If it is not streaming out you, must shut down the engine within about 15 seconds; otherwise, you will burn out the engine. You'll need to remove the cowling (cover for the engine) and determine why the water pump is not working.

Similarly, you cannot run the engine without the lower part of the engine immersed in water. This is because the cooling water pick-up is located at the lower part of the engine. And, as we know, engines without cooling water burn out. If you are testing to see if the engine starts when it is ever out of the water (not advised), always shut down the engine immediately after starting.

Seemingly, each engine has its own distinct personality and requires working with the throttle and choke to get her started and to learn what she likes. Many times it is choke on for two to three pulls and then if she doesn't start—choke off for a few pulls. Once started, you may need to work the choke in and out a little to get her firing smoothly. Did we mention: watch your elbows?

Starter Cord notes: When pulling the cord, start by pulling slowly until you feel resistance. Then give it a good tug. If you just give a yank it without feeling the resistance you will most likely break the cord (eventually), and that is not good. Every few months, pull the cord all the way out slowly and check for any chafing on the cord.

Stopping

The motor will most likely have a "Kill Cord."

This cord is designed to clip around your wrist on one end and clip under the stop button on the other end. If you ever fall overboard, the cord pulls the clip from under the stop button and stops the engine.

Thus, to stop the engine, you can either pull the cord clip out from under the stop button or just push the stop button, hard. After the engine is stopped, ensure it is out of gear. Ideally, you'd put the engine out of gear first, but there is no requirement for that—it's just a good habit to get into so the engine is ready to start next time.

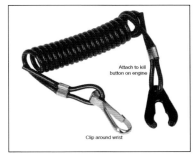

Kill cord.

Line Entanglement

You're motoring along and the engine suddenly stops. Hmmmm—you check the fuel and there is plenty. You take it out of gear, restart the engine (easily), put the engine into gear, and BAM it stops again—you repeat—hmmmmm????

There is a line wrapped around the prop!

This is a reasonably common occurrence. It's thus a good idea to have a sharp knife in your tool kit to cut away the entangled line.

Those Annoying Lines

Once, in New Zealand's Bay of Islands, we were just motoring along and the engine just stopped. We had a stray fishing net caught in the prop. We did not have a sharp knife in the tool kit—or even a dull one, for that matter. We found a shell on the floor of the cockpit, broke it, and used the sharp edge to cut away the nylon.

Several years later, on a yacht charter vacation to Belize, a crew member had taken the dinghy for a "10-minute" blast in the middle of the night. Several hours later, he paddled back and woke me up cussing, saying, "every time I started the engine, it stalled when I put it into gear." In my sleepy state without opening my eyes, I said, "you have a line around the prop." I then rolled over and went back to sleep. I heard him muttering on the way back to the dinghy, "how the hell can he diagnose that?" In the morning, he confirmed my diagnosis.

Reverse

Reverse is always a tricky operation because with the prop pulling the engine backward, the backward thrust wants to pull the engine away from the boat. If you are applying too much throttle, the engine rears up and out of the water, which is pretty scary, embarrassing, and dangerous. Use low throttle when in reverse. On the engine mounting bracket, there is usually a locking clip to prevent the engine from rearing up, but often people forget to engage this locking clip.

Tilt Lifting the Engine

At the bottom of the engine cowling on the mounting bracket is the "Tilt Lift Lock Lever." Engage this after you have tilted your engine out of the water, during storage at the marina, and while you are sailing. Don't tilt the engine up while the engine is running because that brings the water intake out of the water and will burn out your engine.

Tilted engine.

Safety

- Elbows. Elbows. Elbows. Mind those elbows when starting.
- Fuel—make sure that there is no excess fuel spilled on the boat. Wipe with a detergent-soaked rag and remove the rag from the boat.
- Propeller—kinda obvious because a propeller is otherwise known as a BCD—body chopping device. Anytime you are anywhere near people in the water, put the engine in neutral.
- Tilt lift—watch fingers.

The Head

Someone has to talk about it.

The icky yucky continues because someone has to carry the effluent out of the boat, and often.

Fortunately, the bottom tank part clicks off and it is kinda sealed when carrying out.

So here are a few tips:

- In the email you send out to everyone prior to the sailing venture, just say, "There is a small, cramped, relatively nonprivate toilet on board, but I'd suggest taking care of as much business as you can before coming out (including the kids)." That should take care of most of your effluent problems.
- Keep a container of holding tank treatment onboard and/or use those convenient little Toss-Ins.
- Clean the tank out often.
- Encourage a lot of swimming.
- Make available small plastic disposal bags in a dispenser mounted in the head area for putting anything in that should not go into the head. Place a small bin with lid next to the head.
- Make a sign with what you don't want down there—for fun, we've provided one for you to laminate. Download the PDF below.

Please Don't Flush

Tampons
Maxi Pads
Paper Towels
Cigarette Butts
One-Night Stands
Cell Phones
Condoms
Love Letters
Junk Mail
Sweaters
Socks
Hopes
Dreams
Goldfish
Diapers
Make-Up
Wallets
Maps or Charts
Gum
Poetry
Babies
Puppies
Your Ex

Suggested sign for your head.

Chapter 3
Rigging

Introduction

The hull keeps us afloat while the rigging keeps us moving.

This is an interactive image of a typical small keelboat—a Beneteau 20. Tap the QR Code at right and click on the magnifying glass and the blue circles to zoom.

There are literally hundreds of names of thingies on a boat—many of them strange. We don't expect you to remember them all now, but you should get to know them because it helps to communicate with others on a boat. Don't worry, "harden up on the jib sheet" will soon be flowing out of your mouth without thought, like a second language.

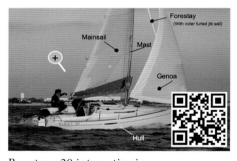

Beneteau 20 interactive image.

Standing Rigging

Some may argue that the boom is part of the standing rigging. Others may not. In any case, by and large, the standing rigging is the mast and anything that holds it up; scan the code at right.

Fractional Rigs

In a fractional rig, the forestay attaches lower on the mast. It is only used when

Standing rigging.

there is an adjustable backstay so you can change the shape of the mainsail when necessary.

The mast is not supported by the forestay above this point, but rather the strength of the mast material is relied upon to prevent the mast from flexing too much or breaking. The backstay will reach all the way to the top. Fractional rigs exist to allow the backstay to be tensioned. This bends the mast and changes the sail shape.

See the animation at right and watch the sail flatten when the backstay is tensioned (tap the green "tension backstay" button). Note that this is an advanced action for sail trim. It's not something you will be doing on your first 10 or even 20 outings.

Masthead Rig

The opposite of a fractional rig is a masthead rig in which the forestay is attached at the top of the mast.

Running Rigging

A sailboat's running rigging consists of those items controlling the sails and helping the sails capture the wind's energy.

Here you find a fascinating array of hardware, all with specialized functions and unique names. Most are quite expensive because they must be uniquely designed and made of reliable non-corrosive materials that will not fail under stress.

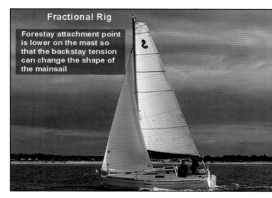

Fractional rig.

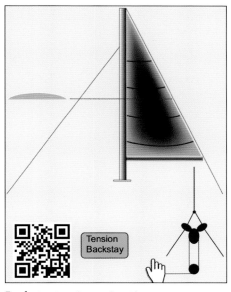

Backstay tension animation.

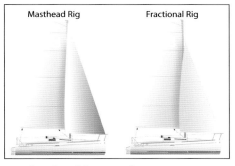

Masthead and fractional rigs.

The main running rigging names you should know are shown here below. Tap the letters on and off so that you can use the animation to test yourself.

A bit of trivia: A sheet is a line that seemingly doesn't make sense until you know that "sheet" comes from the Old-English word "sceata," which means the lower point of the sail. Thus, "tighten the sceata" meant to pull on the line attached to the sceata. The line then became the sceata—which then became "the sheet." Use this piece of trivia to impress your instructor when out on the water.

- The main halyard is used to hoist the mainsail up the mast.
- The Cunningham is used to provide downhaul tension on the mainsail. It usually has multiple blocks so that extra tension can be applied over the ability of the main halyard.
- The boom vang controls the downward tension on the boom, which acts to flatten the mainsail and prevent the boom from rising too much when sailing downwind.
- The mainsheet allows the boom to swing out to capture the wind at various boat angles to the wind.
- The jibsheet flattens the jib sail. The more you head in upwind directions, the flatter the jib should be.

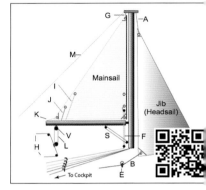

Running rigging terms animation.

- The reefing lines allow the sail to lower a little, which decreases the area size of the sail.
- The jib fairlead changes the downhaul tension on the leech (back) of the jib sail, changing its shape.
- The running backstay is an adjustable backstay for fractional rigs. It changes the shape of the mainsail.
- The traveler moves the mainsheet laterally across the boat. It changes the shape of the mainsail.

If you are lucky, most of the rigging lines run back to the cockpit for easy access.

Hardware

The names and designs and uses of boat hardware are overwhelming. There are cleats, blocks, shackles, and dozens of modifications to each design, all for that one perfect specific use.

The below assortment is just a taste. Rather than have you memorize all the names, it's better that you learn the names from practical experience on boats over years to come. Yes, years!

Department of Redundancy Department

As a guest on a Mediterranean sail between Cannes and Corsica, I asked the captain why he seemed to have replacements for every part of the boat stored somewhere down below. The Captain said merely, "Experience, boy. Experience." He'd sailed the boat around the world for over four years.

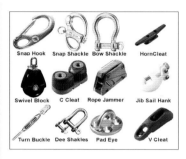

Hardware.

It is important that you constantly check all your boat hardware for corrosion and wear. And in particular, check your turnbuckles. Turnbuckles are on the fore and back stays holding up the mast. They are a means of adjusting the stay tensions (aka tuning the rig). But if they come undone, your mast will come tumbling down with disastrous results worse than Humpty Dumpty. Turnbuckles should be locked at all times with split pins to prevent them from turning.

Lines and Knots

Sailboats seem to be awash in "ropes"—properly called lines by sailors. These lines come in a wide range of materials from some that stretch easily (nylon) to others that are less elastic:

Selecting lines is not simply a matter of what color or thickness you like; these lines serve specific purposes calling for unique characteristics. Here is a partial list of common lines and their functions:

- Halyards—used to raise and lower sails
- Sheets—used to control the mainsail boom and jib (head) sail

- Furling lines—used to furl main and head sails

Some lines may pass through various blocks (pulleys) and adjusting devices, like travelers, and some may end up being controlled by winches. Lines that are subject to abrasion should regularly be inspected and replaced if it appears they have been compromised.

Lines on a boat.

There are, however, at least three ropes on a boat, contrary to many a crusty sailor. This piece of trivia can be used to win libations at the local marina bars:

- **The Bell Rope:** The small rope attached to the ball on a bell.
- **The Bolt Rope:** The sewn-in rope at the leading edge of a sail to hold it in its track.
- **The Bucket Rope:** About 6 ft (2m) long attached to a bucket used for deck washdown.

Caution: when underway, the use of the bucket rope may require the use of a throw line by your crew members. The sudden, unexpected, and strong tug of a bucket filling with water is likely to pull you overboard.

Knots

The art of using lines (rope) to perform many sailing tasks often requires tying knots. Many of these knots are clever indeed and have a long rich history. Sheet bend knots dating back to 7,000 BC have been found in fishing nets in Finland.

Learning to tie knots is both fun and challenging. The bowline, which is a loop that will not close, is well known, but many other knots are equally important, such as the half hitches, sheet bend, splices, and figure eight. Some knots tend to be purely decorative, while others may be essential for survival.

The website http://www.animatedknots.com is by far the best reference for learning to tie knots. The knots are shown in an animated format so you can easily learn the progression. They also have iPhone, iPad and Android apps, which you can use to take with you on a sailing trip and make challenges for the kids (adult kids, too).

iPhone app - Animated Knots

Android app - Animated Knots

Below and on page 46 are the knots you need to know. By clicking on the image, you will be taken to the animated knots' specific knot page.

Bowline

A bowline is typically used to tie the jib sheets to the clew of the jib sail.

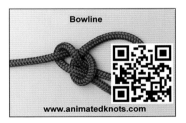

Bowline.

Reef or Square knot

The Reef knot, aka square knot, is mainly used when reefing the sail. This knot is not very secure; it can easily slip undone.

Reef knot.

Round Turn with Two Half Hitches

A round turn with 2 half hitches is typically used to tie to a pylon.

Round turn with two half hitches.

Rolling Hitch

A rolling hitch is used when you need a knot that won't slip when pulled at an angle. This knot is ideal for taking strain off another rope or for not sliding on a pole.

Rolling hitch.

Clove Hitch

The Clove Hitch is quick to tie and easy to adjust. It is ideal for securing fenders (and horses, thus its name).

Clove hitch.

Cleat Hitch

The Cleat Hitch is used to make fast to a cleat.

Cleat hitch.

Figure of Eight

The Figure of Eight knot is easy to tie and stops rope from escaping through a jammer, block, or padeye. It is also very easy to undo when needed.

Figure of eight.

Sails

Sails are undoubtedly the most complex component of any sailboat. They must constantly adjust to a variety of wind conditions. Sails are the essential items, in design and materials, for efficient and safe sailing.

Mastering sail design and sail handling is a lifelong learning experience that involves practice, knowledge, and intuition. Adjusting your sails while trying to anticipate wind shifts is fun indeed.

Every sail on a vessel represents a compromise involving the kind of winds the vessel will encounter, the vessel's displacement, racing or cruising configuration, and finally—perhaps most important—how deep the owner's pockets are. Most sailors are initially quite content with the basic main and headsails provided by the manufacturer.

Sail Nomenclature

The illustration on page 47 shows the parts of the sail and associated control lines. Of note is the bolt rope, which is one of very few actual ropes on a boat (do you remember the other ropes?).

- The bolt rope is usually sewn into the luff (leading edge) of the sail. It provides strength to the luff edge of the sail. If the mast or forestay has a track, then the boltrope slides up inside the track to hold the luff in place. If the sails are "hanked on" with "hanks" (clips), then the boltrope provides reinforcement to the sail so that the hanks do not pull out.
- Hanks are basically sliding clamps that slide up the forestay and are clamped onto the bolt rope at the leading edge (luff).
- The main halyard is attached to the head of the sail and is used to pull the sail up the mast.
- The gooseneck is a swivel connection from the boom to the mast.
- The reefing points are points where the sail can be pulled down in order to reef the sail if a roller furling system is not used.
- The topping lift holds the back of the boom up.
- The boom vang holds the boom down when beating to wind. On downwind legs, the boom vang can be loosened to provide more shape to the sail.
- The Cunningham pulls the sail down tight and is used also when reefing.
- The outhaul line is attached to the clew to pull the sail out along the boom.
- Battens are fiberglass sticks that slot into pockets on the sail to help provide sail shape.

Scan the code below, tap the letters, and test yourself.

Types of Sails

Sails are sophisticated objects. It is not only the materials they are made from that is important, but also the way they are cut and sewn.

Most likely, initially, you will be dealing with a headsail and a mainsail.

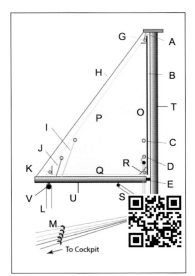

Name of sail terms.

Mainsails

Mainsails are large sails attached to the mast and boom. They fly behind the mast. These sails generally provide the primary propulsion force.

Mainsails often have battens, semirigid fiberglass slats that are inserted into pockets sewn on the sail. Battens help a sail maintain its most efficient shape.

Mainsails are either:

1. Raised up the mast with the main halyard. The luff of the sail is either attached to sliders that move in a track up the mast or by a rope sewn into the luff of the sail and fed into a slot in the mast. The sail in its lowered state is either flaked back and forth over the boom or rolled up inside the boom (boom roller furled).
2. Furled inside the mast and, when ready for deployment, are unfurled by releasing the inhaul line and pulling on the outhaul line to pull or unroll (unfurl) it out of the mast.

The advantage of a boom furling mainsail or traditional raising mainsails is that the sail can have traditional battens in the sail. Battens are designed to give the sail better shape and thus increased lift (sail efficiency). Battens also allow a "roach" in the sail, meaning that the sail leech can be curved out rather than a straight line down from the head to the clew.

Mast furling sails can have battens, but they are sewn into the sail in a vertical direction. Some efficiency is gained but not near as much as horizontal battens.

More than likely on a small keelboat you will be dealing with non-roller furling mainsails. You will need to raise the sail up the mast.

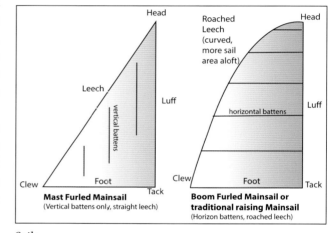

Sails.

Headsails

Headsails are sails used in front of the mast. They may be large (genoa) or small (jib) depending upon the wind strength of the day. The headsail can be hanked (clipped) onto the forestay and raised up using the headsail halyard or furled, whereby it is rolled in around the forestay using outhaul and inhaul lines.

Furling Headsail

Furling headsails are very common these days. They unfurl (unroll) and furl (roll up) around the headstay in a matter of seconds. They are relatively inexpensive to install on the forestay and provide ease of handling for cruisers because there is no need to go up on the foredeck to bring the sail down or raise the sail. There is also no need to change out sails when reefing (putting up a smaller sail due to high wind conditions) because the sail can simply be rolled up incrementally to reef (make the sail smaller) the sail.

Some aerodynamic efficiency is lost when a furling headsail is installed because furling sails lack battens. Battens provide shape to the sail, making it more like the shape of an efficient airfoil. Some sailmakers have provided vertical battens for roller furling systems. This helps some with efficiency, although not 100%. Still, the trade-off in ease of handling versus loss in efficiency is an obvious choice for most. Unless you're aiming to win races, the roller furling headsail is a good choice.

The top code to the right is a video by Harken, which manufactures roller furling systems. It's about 5 minutes long and is a good introduction to using a headsail roller furling system.

The code underneath is another headsail furling video by Profurl, who also build furling systems. This is a more technical explanation on the components of a furling system.

Sail Handling

Sails provide "lift." When a sail is doing its best, it has a concave shape, where the windward side of the sail has a higher pressure than the leeward side. This difference in pressure is the force that propels the sailboat. This is the same aerodynamic force that keeps a plane flying.

Sail handling is the essence of being a sailor. It involves fundamental physics in order to make judgments about the conditions in which you are sailing. This topic is never exhausted and often the source of warm-to-heated discussions.

The most common sail material is probably Dacron, but in addition, sails can be made from Kevlar, Mylar, carbon fibers, and hybrids. Sail manufacturing and design is a highly technical business. Since different areas of a sail are loaded differently by the force of the wind, the design must account for the unique stretching and strength properties of the materials to maintain an efficient aerodynamic shape. However, cost is also a big factor in design because some exotic materials such as carbon and Kevlar fibers can make a sail very (very) expensive. But, expensive sails also help win races.

Trimming sails for maximum lift is a sailor's primary challenge. This trimming is done using lines called sheets (jib and main), and these lines are often tensioned using winches.

Sail handling under a variety of conditions is one of the most challenging tasks facing any sailor or crew. You have to understand and adjust for currents, wind, and sea conditions while simultaneously anticipating what may happen next. In stormy conditions, these decisions may be critical.

The overall object of managing sails is to maintain a power balance on the vessel, ensuring safety and efficient passage. Good vessel balance results from constantly being aware of sea and weather conditions and then making prudent adjustments of sails. If you are sailing in a regatta (race), sail handling and clever helmsmanship are key to winning.

Summary: A modern sailboat's efficiency depends upon sails being skillfully and safely handled to harness the wind for propulsion. Capturing this free and abundant energy source is accomplished by a variety of clever devices, including standing and running rigging along with sails.

When standing rigging has been well tuned, it generally needs only periodic inspections and perhaps occasional minor adjustments.

Sails and rigging should be routinely inspected for wear and tear, and maintained or replaced when necessary. Depending upon the use, it may sometimes be cost-effective to clean the sails. There are a variety of professional services and treatments available.

You never want to lose your ability to control the wind in your sails.

Winches

Using a winch is fundamental to most of us, but the first time you see one it may not be obvious. A winch is the way you wind in the sheets (lines-ropes) nice and tight. It provides hundreds of times the mechanical advantage over what you could apply with your hands, and it will hold the sheet long after you get tired of holding on to it.

Modern winches have a slot around the top. This makes the winch "self-tailing." A self-tailing winch does not require anyone to pull on the sheet as it comes out of the winch. The slot automatically clamps the sheet in so it cannot pull out backwards. You'll need to notice the stainless steel tab that drops down over the slot. Use this tab to bring the sheet up into the top slot. Many people make a mistake of just winding the sheet up into the slot without the tab. This will cause the sheet to undo. Use the tab!

Many winches go in both directions—one for faster winding in and the other direction for slower winding. The slower direction applies more mechanical advantage. So use the fast direction until it gets too tough, then switch to the other direction to wind in the last bit.

Here are the quick secrets:

- No matter what you think—it's always in a clockwise direction that you wrap the sheet (line/rope) around the winch (even in the southern hemisphere).

- The more times you wrap the sheet around the winch, the more friction is applied and the more pulling power you can apply.
- If the sheet is not moving as you turn the winch, wrap it around the winch one more time.
- Usually, most winches are limited to about 4 wraps.
- Under most circumstances, 2 wraps will do.

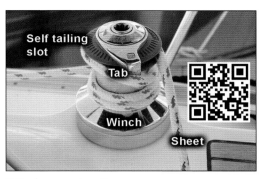

Winch use animation.

- If the wind gets above 12 knots, you'll need 3 wraps.
- Use the tab to get the sheet up into the top slot.
- Keep your fingers clear.

Locking cleats are simple. They simply lock the line from moving back out once you've pulled in. The trick to unlocking is that the lever has to be ALL THE WAY BACK, not half way up. Second, a safety item must be noted here. NEVER just flick the lever open. If there is tension on the line, you or the person holding the line will experience rope burn, which is not a pleasant thing. We all learned this as a child. ALWAYS wind the line around the winch at least two times and cleat it, then flick the lever all the way open, now slowly release the tension on the line. Once the tension is gone, you can remove the line from around the winch.

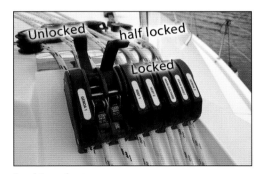

Locking cleats.

Sailing Tip

Watch this video on how to manage the winch handle:

Chapter 4
Rules of the Nautical Road

The Rules

The Rules are the Rules are the Rules. They are internationally agreed upon and are absolute essential knowledge for a skipper. Built into the rules is the requirement to be a responsible seaman (seaperson is more of a PC term, but we're not sure if this is a word; it should be). This means that the rules themselves require knowledge of the rules. Thus, lack of knowledge is not a defense. And neither is just keeping out of the way. In fact, keeping out of the way is dangerous because the other boat is expecting you to behave in a certain way—according to the rules.

The biggest reason people don't study the rules is that they perceive that the study would be incredibly dry (isn't the idea of sailing to get slightly wet?). Thus there is a temptation to put this knowledge off. But what is often misconstrued by those not completely studying the rules is that a person who seemingly had "rights" during a crossing situation is not exonerated from liability if a collision occurs. How is that possible?

Since all of the rules are important and relevant to a sailor, it would be irresponsible for us to just touch on the rules and give you some basics in this book. Fortunately, NauticEd has an excellent, engaging, and interactive course on the Rules online. As a benefit to this book, you are offered and encouraged to take and pass the NauticEd Navigation Rules course online for free. Scan the QR code to the right and sign up for free. The Rules course will automatically be dropped into your curriculum.

You'll find that the study of the rules is rich in history and interest. For example, why do you think that a port tack boat must give way to a starboard tack boat? Could it have equally been the other way around? No—there is a specific reason that was forged in history. Take the FREE online Rules course now and learn why.

Chapter 5
Maneuvering in the Marina

Introduction

This is where we keep the gelcoat on your boat and off the dock, and consequently, your money in your pocket.

The marina is where most accidents occur. Maneuvering is tight and you have to get it exactly right. And as you will learn from this chapter, maneuvering in the marina is NOT the place to learn maneuvering in the marina. Contained here is a set of exercises that you will perform in open waters with some buoys or floating fenders on your boat fitted with an outboard motor.

It's now time for a Latte. Got one? Ok, now let's learn about maneuvering a small keelboat with an outboard motor.

Outboard motor.

Motor Management

There are three dimensions to think about with an outboard motor:

- Turning left and right
- Forward and reverse
- Throttle

Left and right motor turning is easy. You just move the motor tiller arm. Duh!

Forward is also pretty easy. Engage forward and crank the throttle. But don't do that in the opposite order. Changing gears requires idle speed; otherwise, you will strip the gearbox. Even if you are in a panic and collision is imminent, stripping the gearbox out is the last thing you want because it leaves you basically helpless in the marina with a future empty pocket book.

Reverse is a little bit more complicated. With reverse, mistakes and damage can happen. Why? Because if you crank the throttle in reverse too much, the engine wants to climb backwards out of the water, rearing up like a wild bronco. If the engine rears up, keep calm and ease off on the throttle. This will drop the engine back down and you can continue. Bottom line: just don't use too much throttle in reverse. Usually, however, there is a lever lock on the tilt mechanism to prevent the rearing up. But invariably, you or your crew will forget to lock this.

Watch the animation at the bottom of the page to see the above action and worse.

Managing the engine is like a good golf swing. You independently work the throttle, engine tiller left and right, and the gear lever forward-neutral-reverse.

DON'T

- shift gear while the engine throttle is more than idle
- go into high speed on the throttle when in reverse gear
- flick quickly from forward to reverse or reverse to forward
- bring the lower unit (propeller area) out of the water while the engine is running, or else you burn out the water cooling impeller

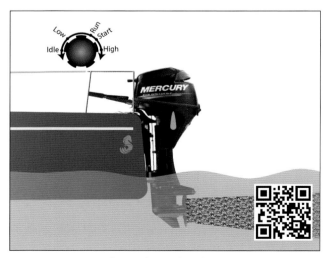

Operation animation.

- bonk people in the face with your elbow when starting
- have the propeller spinning anywhere near human body parts. (Kinda obvious but the attorneys made us write that. Not really. But you can imagine the argument in court: "You failed to make my client aware of the dangers of a spinning piece of metal next to his hand.")

So, left and right, forward and reverse, and throttle are the three dimensions (engineers call it 3 degrees of freedom) of the engine. But regarding maneuvering the boat, there is this other double dimension like a duplicate planet earth hiding behind the sun that we can't see. It is the rudder, because the rudder also turns the boat. Operating both the rudder tiller and the engine tiller simultaneously is difficult because it requires two hands. And two hands is the maximum we have. Most times, then, we just lock the engine tiller or the rudder tiller depending on what operation we are doing.

Be aware that for each type of rudder and engine mounting system there are operational concerns:

- The outboard engine controls may or may not be in easy reach of the helm
- The throttle and turning controls may or may not be able to be locked in a position. Locking controls allow the helmsperson to concentrate on the tiller and forward observations
- Lockable controls can vibrate loose
- The engine may or may not be in a fixed position and cannot be rotated
- The engine may or may not be able to be linked to the rudder (clever, but linkages can be problematic)
- The setup may be such that the propeller can contact the rudder (chomp chomp)
- The engine may be mounted far to one side of the boat, making turning radii vastly different
- An odd combination of any of the above

Each manufacturer has its own designs. So this chapter is written generically to accommodate general operations. Some things presented here may work better for you than others. If you are being taught by an instructor, please don't say, "But NauticEd says to do it this way. . . ." More than likely your instructor is going to know the set-up of your boat the best.

In general, if the engine controls are hard to reach or will not stay locked, you may need to use another crew member to help you operate the engine. The prime directive (Star Trek Language) is that you maintain a vigilant watch so that you are not hitting anything. If your eyes are too much on the engine and other goings on, you're not paying enough attention to the outside world (docks, other boats, swimmers, ducks).

Once you figure out the best way to control the boat, being able to rotate the motor gives outboards a great advantage over inboards when it come to maneuvering in close quarters. With an outboard, you are able to direct the prop's flow of water exactly where it is needed to precisely control the boat.

Exercises: Exorcise

Throughout this chapter, we explain the concept and combine it with real exercises that you should perform on a real boat. For now, however, work all the way through imagining yourself on the boat to gain an understanding of the concepts. At the end of the chapter is a printable document of real on-the-water exercises. Print it, grab a friend and some sandwiches, and head out to practice.

Understanding the concepts combined with practical exercises solidifies your knowledge. Through years of teaching maneuvering under power, we have found this theory-first-then-practice creates the best learning process for you. In doing this and repeating these exercises, you are exorcising bad habits you may have developed in the past. Or if you're new, you'll be maneuvering like an ol' pro shortly.

Exercise zero

In thermodynamics class in engineering school, they taught us the zeroth law of thermodynamics. It is "heat flows from hot to cold." It's called the zeroth law because it's so flipping obvious that it doesn't really deserve a number.

The zeroth exercise here is learning to properly operate the gear lever and throttle so that you are ALWAYS CHANGING GEAR IN IDLE SPEED. Here is the exercise:

Exercise 0:

Start the engine in neutral (watch your elbows). Throttle up the engine, then throttle it down to idle. Put the gear lever into forward and throttle up the engine. Throttle down to idle. Put the gear lever into reverse and throttle up again. Bring it back down to idle and shift into neutral. Repeat this exercise 5 times. And once more for fun.

What you learned

You software ROM burned into your brain and hands how to switch between gears in harmony with the throttle. In doing this, you will exorcise the evil desire to change gears at anything other than idle. You will also probably observe the engine rear up while in reverse, and you'll learn not to panic when this happens.

During this process, listen to the engine and get used to what the pitch of the engine sounds like at different throttle positions. In learning the sound made with each throttle position, you can operate the throttle by ear rather than spending valuable time looking at the throttle handle.

Rudder Tiller v. Engine Tiller

Turning

The boat turns because you are creating a force from the water onto the aft of the boat. The force is created by the directional shift of a volume of water via the rudder or via the propeller.

In using the rudder, the only way you can impart this directional shift to the water is when water is flowing over the rudder, that is, the boat has to be moving through the water. If the boat is not moving, all you are doing is wagging your tail.

When using the engine to turn the boat, you are pushing water left or right from the propeller. This creates the force whether the water is flowing past the boat or not.

This seems obvious but it's worth thinking about because the turning force is proportional to the angle of water changing direction and the volume of water that changes direction. At standstill with a rudder, the angle can be great but there is zero volume (no flow). With an engine, the angle can be great and the volume can be great.

The rudder works by deflecting water flowing over it. As the boat speeds up, the volume of water being deflected can become quite high because the size/area of the rudder is large (therefore, displacing a lot of water). And in fact, the force is actually proportional to the speed of the water squared. So if you double your speed from 2 knots to 4 knots, the turning force goes up 4 times; or if you increase your speed from 2 knots to 8 knots, the turning force goes up 16 times. This is what makes a rudder very effective.

Rudder Tiller

During sailing operations, the engine is tilted up and out of the water. Thus, it is always the rudder tiller that you operate during sailing. The story is different, however, when it comes to operating under engine power.

When going long distances under engine power, it is recommended that you set the engine in a straight forward aligned locked position and steer the boat using the rudder tiller. You can easily do course changes without too much issue. This operating position is more comfortable as the rudder tiller arm is longer and gives you more reach around the cockpit. The rudder is very effective because of your speed through the water.

Engine Tiller

When it comes to needing to maneuver in tight spaces like a marina, where you need lower boat speed and there are obstacles all around, you should consider using the engine tiller. This is because the volume flow of water over the rudder has decreased due to decreased speed, and thus the rudder becomes much less effective.

In some cases, it is recommended that you lock the rudder tiller in a straight forward aligned position and use the engine tiller arm to maneuver the boat. This is suggested because when you turn the engine tiller, you are turning the direction of a large volume of water thrust from the propeller, which gives a far greater response to the turning movements.

In other cases, you may need to turn both the rudder and tiller. The point is to practice to see what works for you best.

Exercise 1a: With the boat stopped and the rudder hard over to one side and the engine pointing straight, throttle up the engine to high for 2 seconds. Observe how much the boat turns.

Exercise 1b: With the boat stopped and the engine turned to one side with the rudder straight, throttle up the engine for 2 seconds. Observe how much the boat turns.

What you learned: Since the boat did not build very much speed in 1a, the boat hardly turned at all. In Exercise 1b, you thrust a lot of water sideways and the boat turned significantly.

Momentum

Imagine that there are two buoys in the water. They are 50 yards (50 meters) apart.

Momentum Exercise

Momentum is the propensity of an object to keep doing exactly what it is doing. If your boat is moving, it wants to keep moving. If it is stopped, it doesn't really want to get moving.

In this exercise, you start to get the feel of what it takes to stop your boat in a straight line. You'll have the engine on and the rudder tiller locked in straight forward position. You'll be working the engine throttle and the gear lever in unison.

Exercise 2: Under power, and going down wind, move toward one of the buoys and stop the boat with the buoy abeam of the boat. You'll invariably overshoot. No problem, though, because you're in deep water and nowhere near a marina.

What you learned: You overshot for two reasons: first, the boat has a massive amount of momentum and second, the wind is pushing you from behind. To do it better next time, put the engine into reverse idle about 8-10 boat lengths back. As the boat begins to slow, gauge whether you should increase the engine speed against the approaching speed of the buoy. Work the engine up and down to ensure you stop in the desired place. Most people make the mistake of putting the engine in reverse too late and then have to overpower the engine at the last minute.

Exercise 3: Repeat exercise 2 above but headed into wind.

What you learned: You still run the possibility of overshooting: again, this is because of the momentum of the boat. But you probably didn't overshoot as much because the wind helped slow down the boat. The exact same principles apply. Use reverse to slow the boat with plenty of space, and work the engine to gauge your approach.

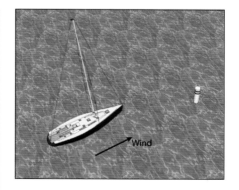

Momentum downwind.

The bottom line here is that the boat does not slow very well in reverse. For another example, try this: from standstill, notice the acceleration of the boat in both forward and reverse. You'll see that the boat takes off much faster in forward. Why? Well that's easy: because the propeller is mostly used in forward, the shape of the prop is engineered to have its greatest efficiency in forward. The tradeoff is poor performance in reverse.

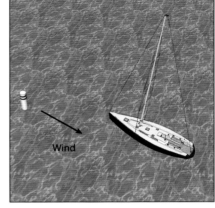

Momentum upwind.

Maneuvering in Forward

Here, you're going to run the boat through its paces going forward at both slow and fast throttle speeds to get the hang of turning radii and maneuvering into a slip.

First, learn the difference between operating with the engine tiller and the rudder tiller.

Exercise 4a: Lock the engine in a center position. Bring the engine to idle and shift into forward. Bring the engine to a medium run speed and lock the throttle. Use the rudder tiller to steer the boat.

Exercise 4b: Lock the rudder tiller to a center position. With the engine running in forward, steer the boat with the engine tiller.

What you learned: Both are good ways for operating the boat. Notice that using the rudder tiller and the engine tiller both produce quite different results.

Learn about how the boat can turn very tight circles using the engine tiller.

Exercise 5a: Position the boat abeam of a buoy and about half a boat length away. Lock the rudder tiller straight forward. Check for traffic! Now put the engine tiller hard over and do 5 donuts around the buoy at high throttle speed. Yippee! Repeat with another 5 donuts in the opposite direction.

Exercise 5b: Repeat at low idle speed

What you learned: You'll see that the boat turns in an extremely tight circle. Not much larger than the length of the boat. You'll see that on a windy day the track of the boat is not affected by the wind. At idle speed on a windy day, you'll notice that the circle diameter is larger and you have much less turning control. You may notice that the boat turns better in one direction than the other.

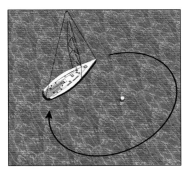

Circles in forward.

Exercise 6a: Repeat the above with the engine locked straight and turn using the rudder at high and low engine speeds.

Exercise 6b: Repeat the above with both the rudder and engine working in unison to turn the boat, i.e., both tillers hard over.

What you learned: You'll notice that the boat can almost turn around with a radius almost its own length when you use both rudder and engine, i.e., an extremely tight circle. You'll also notice that you have two hands tied up.

The downside effect of turning the boat under high engine power is that you continue to gain boat speed, which is not what you want in a marina.

Exercise 7a: With the boat lying still and pointing downwind, and the engine in neutral, first turn the engine tiller hard over. Then engage forward and increase the throttle to high for 2 seconds and back to idle.

Exercise 7b: Repeat but only increase the throttle a little.

What you learned: You'll see that the boat turns very fast but does not gain any appreciable forward speed. At lower throttle speed, you'll see that the boat does not turn as fast. In fact, on a windy day, you may not be able to turn the boat up into wind at all. If there was a boat in front of you, you'd probably hit it. Revving the engine for 2 seconds shoots a large quick volume of water sideways to give you a burst of control. This method should be used in most situations to gain greater control of the boat. You'll also notice that when sitting on one side of the boat, it is easier to control the gear lever.

Exercise 8: To gain an appreciation of control of the boat, do figure 8's around 2 buoys that are spaced close to each other—or just use some imaginary buoys. As you begin the turn, increase the throttle to high and then back down to medium as you come out of the turn, then straighten up to approach the next buoy.

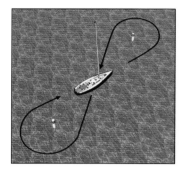

Figure 8.

What you learned: Doing figure 8 exercises will give you a good feeling on how to maneuver and control the boat in forward gear.

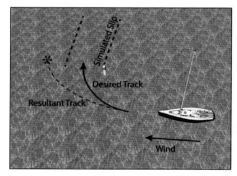

Maneuver into an imaginary slip.

Exercise 9a: Maneuver into an imaginary slip. Pretend you are going to maneuver into a slip as follows. Use the buoy and imagine the slip. You have a strong wind from behind you.

What you learned: You'll probably overshoot on the resultant track and cause some pretty big damage because the momentum of the boat with the force of the wind will carry you past your intended track.

Exercise 9b: Do the same exercise but turn a circle to align you into the slip as follows:

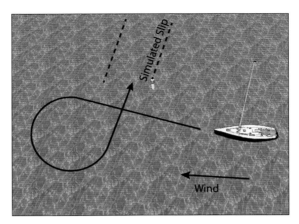

Maneuvering into an imaginary slip with circle.

What you learned: This is the best way to get into a slip with a strong following wind.

Maneuvering in Reverse

A simple rule of thumb for steering a boat backwards: if you want the back of the boat to go one way, point the tiller (rudder or engine) that way.

Maneuvering in reverse intimidates the heck out of most people. But actually, once mastered, it is the easiest gear in which to maneuver. The difficulty is that the rudder can be a real problem. Because the fulcrum (pivot point) of the rudder is at the forward edge, whenever you are going backwards, the rudder will want to swing hard in one direction, thereby slamming the tiller over and potentially breaking stuff. So, you must keep the rudder under control at ALL times; this means tight, constant, and diligent control. If you ever let the rudder tiller go—SLAM. It's the same reason car doors have their hinges at the forward end of the door. Imagine going 60 miles an hour (100km/hr) backward and opening the car door—SLAM.

To keep control of the rudder, you will either keep it in your hand while the other hand is maneuvering the engine tiller, or you have locked the rudder tiller tight in a straight center position.

We keep repeating this, but it is important: When shifting from forward into reverse and vice versa, ALWAYS stop in neutral for 1-2 seconds before shifting gears. Drifting in a marina under high winds and a sheared-out transmission is not something you want to experience. Scared? Don't be; just don't shift the gear lever fast.

Exercise 10a: With the boat stopped and positioned stern to the wind, just hang out for 30 seconds or so and observe the boat's behavior.

Exercise 10b: With the boat stopped and the bow pointed to the wind, just hang out for 30 seconds or so and observe the boat's behavior.

What you learned: Sitting there with your stern to the wind is a stable position for the boat to be in. The wind really does nothing to the boat and you can hang out like this for a while. This is especially true in a marina when you are waiting for other boats to clear out or deciding which slip to go into.

Conversely, with the bow pointed to the wind, the wind tries to push the bow downwind. This is a difficult way to wait for a ferry to clear the terminal.

Therefore, whenever you need to hang out, just point your stern to the wind.

Exercise 11: With the boat stopped and pointing downwind, throttle up the engine in reverse for about 2 seconds. Be careful not to have the engine rear up backward.

What you learned: The boat is not nearly as responsive as the same exercise in forward. In fact, it is doubtful that anything actually happened. This is because the propeller is engineered to be most efficient in forward gear.

Exercise 12: With the boat stopped and pointing downwind, throttle up the engine in reverse and continue backing straight for 50 yards (50 meters). (Ensure the rudder tiller is controlled.)

What you learned: The boat easily moves its stern into the wind and it is easy to maintain a straight line. The boat facing downwind is a stable way to start backing straight.

Exercise 13: While backing in a straight line stern to the wind, experiment with little engine tiller movements. Keep the rudder tiller straight and locked. Get the feel for the boat movements. Experiment with different engine speeds.

What you learned: The boat is quite responsive to engine tiller movements, especially at higher engine speeds. The maneuverability is not dependent on the boat speed, just the engine speed. The propeller instantly thrusts water in a sideways direction, making the stern movement almost instant.

Exercise 14: Repeat exercise 13, but keep the engine tiller straight and move instead the rudder tiller. Experiment at different boat speeds.

What you learned: At low boat speeds it takes a while for the boat to respond. At high boat speeds the boat stern is keen to move and there is a lot of pressure on the rudder tiller. The maneuverability is dependent on the boat speed, not the engine speed. This is where you will really get a feel for the rudder wanting to slam over. Maintain control.

Exercise 15: Repeat exercise 14 but use both the tiller and the engine tiller in unison.

What you learned: The boat is very responsive. But, both of your hands are kept very busy.

Exercise 16: Lock the rudder tiller straight. While backing up into the wind at higher throttle, move the engine tiller to starboard. Allow the boat to do a complete circle.

What you learned: You'll notice that the boat begins to turn quite easily and the radius of turn is again surprisingly tight.

Exercise 17: Repeat Exercise 16 except with the engine tiller to port. Allow the boat to do a complete circle.

What you learned: You'll notice that the boat begins to turn quite easily and the radius of turn is again surprisingly tight. If the engine is mounted on one side of the boat, the turn radii will be different.

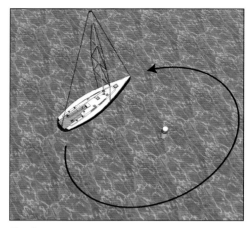 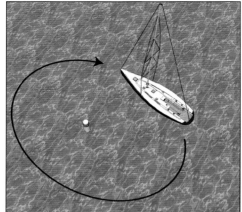

Circles in reverse.   Circles in reverse, other direction.

Exercise 18: Experiment with turning circles at different throttle settings.

What you learned: You notice that on a really windy day at low engine speeds, you may be unable to achieve a complete circle. This is because at the part of the circle where you are bringing the stern downwind, the wind force pushing the bow downwind may equal the engine force pulling the stern downwind. At higher engine speeds, this can be overcome.

The point: Do not be afraid to use engine rpm.

Exercise 19: Lock the rudder tiller. Pick a buoy and do 5 donuts around the buoy in reverse, using the engine tiller at high throttle speed. Adjust the engine tiller position so you don't hit the buoy but keep the boat as close to the buoy as possible. Then straighten out the tiller and back up straight with the wind abeam.

What you learned: You'll notice it is relatively easy to back the boat around like this and even with the wind abeam, you can hold a straight course.

Exercise 20: With the rudder tiller locked straight, do figure 8s around 2 buoys leaving the engine at high throttle speed. Use imaginary buoys if none are present. The figure 8 should be about 5 boat lengths.

What you learned: You should begin to gain confidence in how the boat maneuvers under power going backwards.

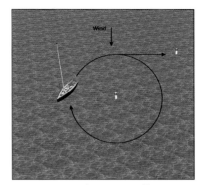

Maneuver with engine tiller.

Now it's time to start to learn how to back into a slip. But we'll first start it outside the marina and next to a buoy. Use the buoy as reference and your imagination to create the docking scenarios below.

Exercise 21: Pretend you're backing up to a dock. With your boat positioned downwind from a buoy, back up to the buoy and stop the boat so that the buoy is positioned 4 feet off the back of the boat. Use forward gear as you get close to the buoy.

What you learned: The boat stops extremely fast. In fact, if you use too much forward, you'll find yourself driving back downwind and away from the "dock" that you're supposed to be tying off to. You'll probably notice that just a spurt of power in forward will do the trick to stop the boat in position. Repeat the exercise so that you can stop the boat effectively in the correct position.

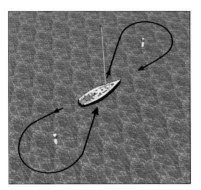

Figure 8s with engine tiller.

Exercise 22: Repeat the exercise from an upwind position and again with crosswind.

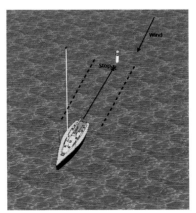

Reversing into an imaginary slip.

What you learned: Here is a crucial learning point: From an upwind position and with crosswind, if you stopped too early and try to start going backwards again, you're going to be forced off course by the wind on your bow at the exact point where it is imperative to keep straight. So it's important to not stop too early, as you will have absolutely no control. What this means is that you must practice practice practice backing downwind and stopping at the right point—every time. Get used to how much power it takes to stop the boat and exactly when you should apply that power.

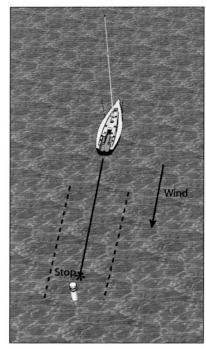

Reversing into an imaginary slip downwind.

Exercise 23: Assume you want to back into a downwind facing slip. Pretend the buoy is the pylon next to your slip. Start with the boat facing downwind, begin backing, and do a U-turn and back the boat into the slip.

What you learned: This is a simple maneuver that could have been troublesome without starting facing downwind (stern to the wind). Remember: we're trying to teach you to always start with your stern to the wind.

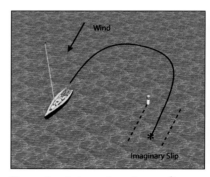

Reversing into an imaginary slip.

So Now You Get It, Right?

To summarize:

- Always begin with your stern to the wind. Then maneuver your boat backwards into the position you want by doing right angle turns, U-turns, or backing straight in.

- Don't stop the boat unless you're either tied off or your stern is to the wind.
- Don't be afraid to use plenty of power.
- If you have to stop and wait for traffic, then do it with your stern to the wind.

And if you can only remember one thing from this entire course: **it is stern to the wind.**

Leaving the Dock

Wisely, you learned to maneuver the boat under power away from the marina, docks, sharp objects, ducks, and other people's boats. Now you're ready to understand how to get out of a tight marina based on various wind and current scenarios.

Leaving the Dock

Before pushing off:

- Assess the wind and current direction at the slip so you can be prepared to keep control of the vessel under the prevailing conditions.
- Make your exit plan.
- Start engine and ensure it is adequately warmed.
- Ensure everything is stowed.
- Make sure there are no dock lines are in the water to tangle the prop.
- Center the tiller.
- Remind guests who do not have assigned jobs to be seated.
- Give clear instructions to each crew member of their coming tasks.

The following diagrams show you how to use wind and current to your advantage.

END TIES

1. Wind pushing you away from the dock.

This is the simplest scenario.
Once you are confident of your plan and traffic is clear:
Release and stow dock lines

- the wind to push the boat clear of other obstacles
- Engage the gear lever

- Use enough power to overcome the effects from the wind. Head out to enjoy the day

2. Wind coming from behind.

This is a little trickier. If you try to go out forwards, the wind could potentially push you into other boats. Additionally, as you turn the tiller to head out, the

Leaving a slip.

rear of the boat will swing around toward the dock and other boats.

There are two ways to do this:

1. turn the engine tiller toward the dock and engage reverse. The engine will pull the aft of the boat out and away from the dock; or
2. you can use a forward spring line

To use a spring line:

- Appoint a crew member to use a fender at the front of the boat to prevent the boat from touching the dock.
- Release and stow the dock lines, but leave one spring line from the dock near the center of the boat attached to the front of the boat.
- The spring line should be arranged so that it is attached to the forward cleat, runs freely around the dock cleat, and returns back to the appointed crew member.

In this manner, the crew member can release the line and retrieve it by letting it slip around the dock cleat. ENSURE that there are no knots in the line to get caught on the dock cleat as it runs through.

- Turn the tiller away from the dock and engage forward gear. This will have the effect of pushing the rear of the boat away from the dock.
- Once the boat has turned out from the dock, straighten the tiller and engage reverse, and have your forward crew member release and retrieve the spring line.

Leaving the dock.

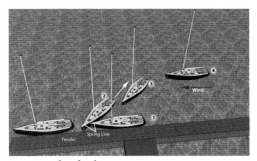

Leaving the dock.

- Continue backing out to be completely clear before engaging forward gear. Remember the rear of the boat will swing back toward the dock once you engage forward and turn the wheel to windward, so ensure there is plenty of room.

3. Wind pushing into the dock and current from behind.

You can use exactly the same methods as described in method 2 above.

4. Wind pushing you onto the dock and current coming from forward.

You will have to balance current and wind a little depending on the strength of each.

If the wind is light, you can usually get away with just pushing the front of the boat out. But significant wind may prevent this from happening and you may need to resort to backing out, as in method 3 above.

Once you are confident of your plan and traffic is clear:

- Appoint a crew member to use a fender at the rear of the boat to prevent the boat from touching the dock.
- Release and stow the dock lines but leave one spring line from the dock near the center of the boat attached to the rear of the boat.
- The spring line should be arranged so that it is attached to the rear cleat, runs freely around the dock cleat, and returns back to the appointed

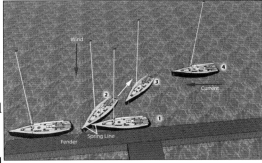

Leaving the dock.

Leaving the dock.

crew member. In this manner, the crew member can release the line
and retrieve it by letting it slip around the dock cleat. ENSURE that
there are no knots in the line to get caught on the dock cleat as it runs
through.

- Turn the engine tiller to open water and engage reverse gear. This will have
  the effect of pulling the front of the boat away from the dock
- Once the boat has turned out from the dock, engage forward gear and have
  your crew member release and retrieve the spring line. Remember, the rear
  of the boat will swing back toward the dock if you turn the tiller. Ensure the
  boat has swung out enough so that you can motor straight out.
- Continue maneuvering out to be completely clear before turning.

Slips

5. Wind coming into the slip channel. Your boat is stern to.

This is best handled by steering out of the slip and then immediately downwind. Back
out of the slip channel and well into the main channel before engaging forward.

6. Wind blowing into the slip channel. Your boat is bow to.

Simply back out of the slip into the slip channel and then into the main channel.
You may need a bow line to the windward dock to prevent the bow blowing downwind as you engage reverse.

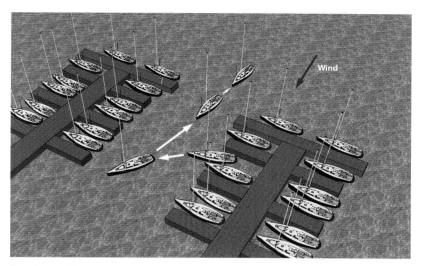

Leaving a slip.

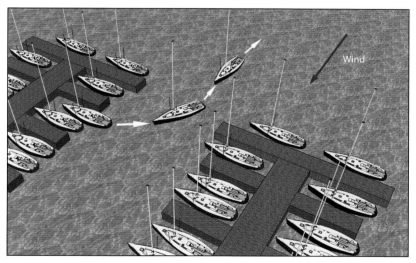

Leaving a slip.

7. Wind blowing out of the slip channel. Your boat is bow to.

Back out into the wind and then engage forward. Watch for traffic as you enter the main channel.

In higher winds you may need to use some lines to assist. View this animation.

Leaving a slip.

Leaving a slip.

8. Wind blowing out of the slip channel. Your boat is stern to.

Simply drive the boat out into the main channel.

9. Wind blows across the docks. Your boat is stern to.

Again, simply drive the boat out into the main channel.

Leaving a slip.

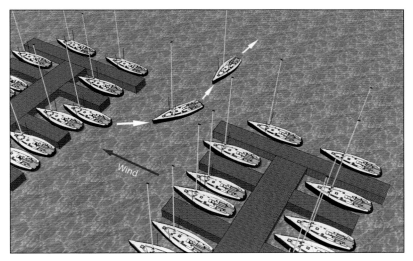

Leaving a slip.

10. Wind blows across the dock. Your boat is bow to.

Simply reverse the boat out of the slip into the slip channel and then into the main channel. If the wind is light, you may elect to turn the boat in the slip channel and come out in forward. However, if the wind is strong, it's safer to follow the above diagram.

Other wind/current configurations are solved using variations of the above techniques.

Always make certain traffic is clear prior to leaving the dock.

Returning to the Dock

Time flies when you are sailing, but sadly, the moment comes when it is time to return and put your vessel back in its slip.

The following are scenarios to help you maneuver your boat back to the dock in a safe and unscratched manner (better known as "no-damage docking").

END TIES

1. Wind blowing you off the dock.

Plan a fairly steep approach so that you are facing more into the wind. Ensure your speed is just adequate to overcome the effects from the wind. Ensure dock lines have been placed on the front and rear of the boat well before you enter the marina. Appoint crew members for tying off. Ensure you instruct your crew members not to jump to the dock, but to step off once the boat is at the dock.

- Aim toward the point on the dock where you want the center of the boat to end up. Usually you can put it out of gear about here.
- Round out just before the dock. Engage reverse.
- Using a combination of reverse and forward, neatly slide the boat to the dock with zero forward speed. You'll need to have your crew members act smartly to get the boat tied to the dock. In high wind conditions you should use a spring line from the front of the boat to the center dock cleat. You can then easily turn the engine tiller toward the dock and engage forward. This will drive the rear of the boat to the dock. Use a fender on the front.

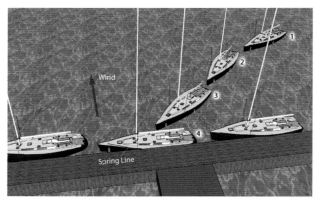

Returning to dock.

Often times, you'll be coming into a fuel dock or pump out station. View the animation at right to get into a tight spot.

2. Wind blowing you onto the dock.

The approach is similar to the above; however, it is a little flatter and your round out is earlier.

3. Wind from behind.

This has the potentially dangerous consequences of pushing you into other boats. It is therefore recommended that you back in.

Returning to dock.

- Place yourself downwind and facing down wind. Engage reverse
- Back the boat toward the point on the dock where you want the center of the boat to end up
- Round out and touch forward if needed to stop the reverse momentum. Ensure that the first dock line to be attached to the dock is the rear one

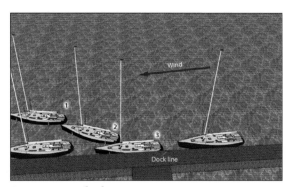

Returning to dock.

Play the animation to the right. This shows how to make your boat go sideways to the wind using the wind as your friend and a combination of power and rudder to keep a balance.

Slips

4. Wind coming into the slip channel. Your boat is to be docked stern to.

Steer into the slip channel and maneuver past the slip. Engage reverse and back up into the wind. Then turn into your dock.

Returning to a slip.

5. Wind blowing into the slip channel. Your boat is to be docked bow to.

Simply steering the boat into the slip works for light wind. However, the below method is safer for stronger winds.

It is preferable to steer the boat up into the wind and into the slip.

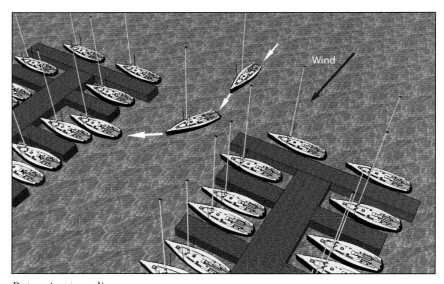

Returning to a slip.

6. Wind blowing out of the slip channel. Your boat is to be docked bow to.

Simply steer the boat into the slip.

7. Wind blowing out of the slip channel. Your boat is to be docked stern to.

Returning to a slip.

Back from the main channel into the slip channel and into your slip.

8. Wind across the docks. Your boat is to be docked stern to.

Back from the main channel into the slip channel and into your slip.

Returning to a slip.

9. Wind blows across the dock. Your boat is to be docked bow to.

Steer the boat into the slip.

Returning to a slip.

Practical Exercises

Well that's it! You're an expert, right? Not! Because you haven't yet gone out and done it and practiced it and practiced it again.

Here is what to do next: check the forecast for a gorgeous windy day that is upcoming. Then call a friend and coax him or her into coming out for a practice training session. On the day, make some sandwiches, grab a few libations (non-alcoholic), and head out. Take this book and go through all the exercises.

We guarantee you'll have a great and memorable day with your friend.

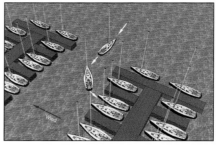

Returning to a slip.

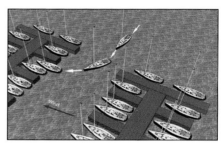

Returning to a slip.

Chapter 6
Sailing

Introduction

This is the chapter you've been waiting for. As you've seen so far, there is a lot more to learn than raising the sail and having the wind take over. But for now, the waiting is over—let's learn the finer points of sailing the boat.

A benefit to this book is the FREE online NauticEd Basic Sail Trim course.

The course will take you about 2 hours to complete. It is loaded with interactive animations and is a great way for you to gain additional knowledge on sail trim. Please enjoy this additional benefit.

The secret of efficient and safe sailing consists of many things, but some primary factors emerge. They include:

- Confidence in your capabilities
- Knowledge of your instruments and boat systems
- Condition of your vessel—including safety gear
- Weather—especially wind direction and strength
- Destination—where you want to go and the weather in transit
- Handling and managing lines smartly and safely
- Crew capabilities and passenger safety and enjoyment
- Your skills as a leader of the crew

Pay close attention. This chapter is the crux of many of the points above.

Did you know that at a young age we were all sailors? Even if you can't remember, we bet you had a rubber ducky; while the real job was supposedly to get clean in the bathtub, you were happy playing for hours with your yellow friend.

Now your former bathtub has become a river, lake, or ocean and your ducky has grown into a fiberglass marvel.

There is a rush that comes from sailing that you never get over. The feeling is one of freedom, adventure, and enthusiasm.

The video to the right is a Beneteau 25 going through its paces. It's just to get you in the mood.

Directions

Directions are super important because while sailing, you will always be in communication with others regarding directions of obstacles, wind changes, your destination, water current, and other boat traffic. Directions are stated in many ways, and so it is important to not only understand them but to communicate them to others in the proper manner. The terminology is important to learn now or else you'll be ultra-confused on the boat.

Port/Starboard

When facing forward, the port side is on the left and the starboard side is on the right. If you look at the front of any boat, you will see a red light on the port side and a green light on the starboard side. These colors are by convention and are the same on every boat in the world. To remember this, use the mnemonic:

"Is there any red port left?"

Upwind and Downwind

You'll see and hear the terms "upwind" and "downwind" a lot, and some confusion can set in.

The term "upwind" can mean ANY direction that is toward the direction the wind comes from. It does not have to be directly into the wind. Thus, 45 degrees upwind means 45 degrees off from where the wind is coming from. "Downwind" can mean ANY direction that is toward where the wind is going. Thus, 135 degrees downwind means 135 degrees off from where the wind is

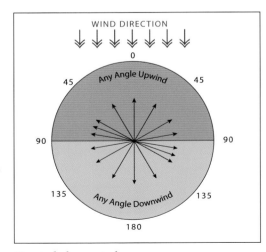

Upwind, downwind.

coming (and it is toward a downwind position). 180 degrees downwind is directly downwind.

Angles to the wind are stated as zero through 180 (many times the word degrees will be omitted). Zero is into the wind directly. 180 is directly downwind. Any angle less than 90 degrees is "sailing upwind." Any angle that is greater than 90 is "sailing downwind." There is no angle greater than 180 in this form.

Heading Up and Bearing Away

Heading up or coming up means turning the boat upwind.

Bearing away or coming down means turning the boat downwind.

Thus, a skipper may say "I'm bearing away to 135 degrees downwind" or "I'm bearing away to 135 degrees off the wind." This would mean that the skipper is turning the boat so that it is sailing downwind 135 degrees away from where the wind is coming.

Head-to-Wind

Head-to-wind is a direction directly into the wind.

Luffing

When the boat is headed too far into the wind for the set of the sail, the sails will start to flap at the leading edge (the Luff edge of the sail). This is called Luffing. When you are head-to-wind, the sails will be flapping wildly like a sheet on a clothes line. To fix this, bear away to fill the sail or tighten the sail sheets. A tactician might say, "bear away, you are luffing." Or the skipper might say, "come in on the mainsheet, the main is luffing".

Luff-Up

Luff-Up means to bring the boat head-to-wind. Consequently the sails will luff. A crew member might ask the skipper to Luff-Up so that a tangle in the jib sheet may be released. Or a tactician might ask the helmsperson to Luff-Up to slow the boat at a race start.

Now you know what this means: "You luffed-up head to wind. Your sails are luffing. Bear away to 40 degrees to starboard off the wind."

Angles Relative to the Boat

Often angle directions are given relative to the boat. Zero degrees is always toward the front of the boat. A skipper might say, "watch out for that rock 60 degrees off our port side." In this case, the direction has nothing to do with the wind direction. It means that if you are looking forward toward the front of the boat and then turn left 60 degrees, you will see the rock.

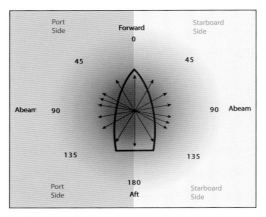

Relative angles.

The tactician might say, "come up 10 degrees." This means relative to the boat heading now, turn the boat in an upwind direction 10 degrees. "Bear away 30" would mean turn the boat 30 degrees downwind from where it is now but keeping the wind on the same side of the boat (i.e., no tack or gybe for this). To get a feel for these degree changes, just think about how 90 degrees would be off your shoulders when looking straight forward. 30 degrees is 1/3 of that. See the clock positions below.

To make directional changes, ALWAYS pick a spot on land or something (a cloud, a boat, a buoy) that is approximately where the direction change is, then after you have picked it, make your change toward that or relative to that. Otherwise, you will begin your turn and not accurately know where to stop turning. Getting your direction changes wrong is a good way to get the helm taken from you by someone more competent.

In addition, a tactician may give you an angle in an o'clock manner. For example, "do you see see that boat at 3 o'clock?" These angles are also always stated relative to the front of the boat no matter what direction you are headed, 12 o'clock being the front (bow) of the boat and 6 o'clock being the back (aft) of the boat.

While pretty obvious to most, we'll show a graphic for the benefit of those brought up in the digital age only.

The o'clock description of directions is highly convenient and often used. There is no need to state port or starboard and for most of us, it is intuitive.

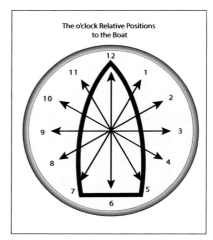

Relative to the clock.

In all other cases, angles and directions are given with the label distinction "upwind" or "downwind," OR "port" or "starboard," so you can distinguish if the angle is measured from where the wind is coming or relative to the boat.

These are examples of valid angle commands or observations using port or starboard relative to the boat:

- 90 degrees to port
- A boat is at 130 degrees on our port
- A rock is abeam to starboard (abeam is 90 degrees)
- There is a buoy in the water at 1 o'clock 100 meters out

These are valid directions, commands, or observations using wind angles:

- Come up to 30 degrees off the wind
- Bear away to 120 degrees off the wind
- There is a boat downwind of us
- Tack and then bear away to 45 degrees off the wind

Compass Directions

Another set of directions used is compass directions. This is more fully covered in Chapter 8, Navigation.

A skipper may tell the helmsperson, "make your course 270 degrees on the compass." This is referring to sailing the boat in a direction toward 270 degrees (270 degrees is west).

Compass directions are all about the compass and have nothing to do with the current boat heading or the wind or the clock.

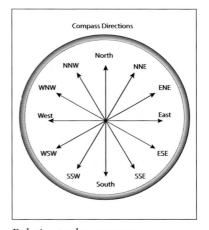

Relative to the compass.

Windward and Leeward

Windward refers to any direction toward the wind. Leeward (pronounced *loo-ward*) refers to any direction downwind. Thus, a Lee shore is a shore that is downwind. The windward side of the boat is the side closer to where the wind is coming from. A boat to leeward means a boat that is in a more downwind position from you (though not necessarily directly downwind). Remember this from the Rules: a leeward boat is the stand-on vessel when both boats are on the same tack.

The High-Side and the Low-Side

When the boat heels over it creates a high-side to windward and a low-side to leeward. Typically the helmsperson sits on the high side of the boat to help balance the heeling force from the wind. Many times the crew are placed "on the rail" (the high side) and told to think of fat thoughts of hotdogs and hamburgers to further counterbalance the heeling force.

High and low side.

Don't Be Scared

Why a Sailboat Does Not Tip Over!

The animation on page 87 shows the balance of forces: actually it is technically the balance of a concept called "moments." First off then, we'd better explain moments. Simply explained: if you hold your hand out straight and someone puts a pound weight in your hand, it is harder to hold than if they put the same pound on your elbow. Even easier— if they put the pound weight right by your shoulder, it's the same pound weight, but it was the "moment" that was straining your muscles, not the weight. Moment, then, is weight multiplied by distance (nothing to do with moment in time).

Heeling over.

- What tends to tip the boat over is the moment of the wind force high up in the sails.
- What tends to right the boat back is the keel weight and the distance it is off center.

Now watch the animation 10 times over or so and watch each dynamic as it is happening. Then refer to the text below, which will further explain . . .

Use the green "incr. wind" button. This interactive animation is best observed using Google Chrome browser.

The force on the sails is the pressure multiplied by the area on the sails on which the wind is acting. The pressure is proportional to the velocity of the wind squared. Why? It just is! It's one of those formulas that makes up the universe.

And from above, the moment is the force multiplied by the height of the position where the wind is considered to singularly act. This position is called the center of the pressure (COP). The center of pressure is the position on the sail whereby if we replaced all the wind all over the sail with an equal force at some position, that would be the position called the center of pressure. On a right triangle sail the point is 1/3 of the way up the mast starting at the boom.

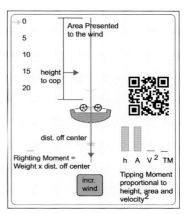

Balance of moments animation.

So the tipping moment is proportional to area, height, and wind speed squared.

So what really happens is this: the wind tips the boat over a bit and this shifts the keel weight off centerline a bit. The boat will continue to heel over until the tipping moment by the wind is equal to the moment from the keel being off center. At this point, the boat will stop heeling over farther and the moments are balanced.

Now the wind picks up again, and again the boat heels over farther and the keel does some righting. But also notice that the area of the sail presented to the wind has reduced and the height to the COP has also reduced. So as the boat heels: area and height decrease on the tipping side of the equation.

At all times, for the boat to not continue to heel farther, the moments of tipping and righting have to be balanced.

This equation must balance: keel weight x distance = area x height x vel².

The only dynamic input to the system is the wind. Everything else in the equation is just working to balance the velocity squared.

So the heel of the boat is purely balancing the wind force on the rig. Duh! While you knew that, perhaps you had not seen it in equation form.

Now go back and run the animation some more. Notice that the two moments are always in balance.

To further extrapolate: when the boat heels way way way over, there is almost no sail area presented to the wind, and the height (h) has reduced also. Additionally, the keel distance off center has moved way out, which is acting to pull the keel down (boat upright) again.

So next time you're out there and the boat heels way way way over, don't worry; every little thing is going to be all right. You've got mathematical equations working in your favor. Area and height are reducing, and keel distance off center is increasing.

Best you check the keel bolts every now and again however! Yup, the keel dropping off would be a problem!

Points of Sail

Wind Vane

Just like a speedometer on your car, your boat has an instrument you must check often (very often) to see how you are doing in relation to the wind. Overspeed in your car at the wrong place, and you get a ticket. Sail at nonoptimal sail set with respect to the wind, and your crew are going to admonish you. If you're racing and you are the sail trimmer or helmsperson, you're going to get a tongue-lashing from the tactician.

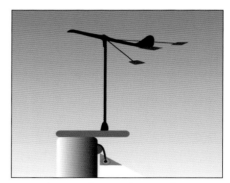

You will be checking this instrument every 4 to 10 seconds depending on what the wind is doing—varying, gusting, or changing direction: veering (changing clockwise) or backing (changing counterclockwise).

Here it is—it's called a wind vane. It sits on top of the mast and points to where the wind is coming from.

A windvane tells you the wind's direction.

Looking directly down onto the wind vane, if you are pointing directly into the wind it will look like the diagram to the right.

Or if you are sailing along and the wind is coming from, say, 45 degrees off your starboard side, it will look like the diagram on the next page.

The arrow always points to the direction of the apparent wind. The two bright red tails are stationary and indicate that if the darker red tail of your arrow is in this zone, you are sailing too close into the wind. You can only sail your boat efficiently if the red tail of the arrow is outside the two red stationary tabs.

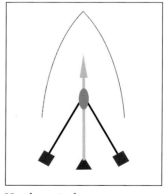

Head to wind.

Now hear this: just like steering your car, you would NOT keep looking at your speedometer while you accelerated to 60 miles per hour (100km/hr). You'd be off the road in a ditch. What you do is glance at your speedometer for 1/2 second or so as you approach your target speed.

The same principle applies: DO NOT look at your wind vane for any longer than 1/2 second each time. Keep your eyes on the water and land so that you are sailing in a straight line. When you want to make a direction adjustment, check the wind vane first (1/2 second), then bring your eyes back to the land. Now make a relative adjustment to the land

Sailing at 45 degrees.

and then check your wind vane for 1/2 second to see if you made the correct adjustment. Repeat if necessary. You simply can not make direction adjustments while looking at the wind vane. You will overshoot your mark EVERY time no matter how experienced you are.

However, because every novice makes this mistake, we will just repeat it. DO NOT look at your wind vane for any longer than 1/2 second and do not watch the wind vane while you are making direction changes. Just don't do it: EVER.

Points of Sail

Points of Sail is a term used to describe the angle the boat is headed relative to the wind. Initially as a novice, it is not that easy to determine; but it becomes easier with experience. At all times, you must know your Point of Sail because this determines how you set your sails.

Novices can tell you that the wind is coming from the left side of the boat or the right side. But if you ask them to state the angle relative to the boat, they clam up. That's ok—this is all new.

Fortunately, the wind vane tells you almost exactly what is going on at all times. And now, armed with the knowledge of the wind angle and thus the Point of Sail, you can set your sails almost perfectly.

For every angle to the wind you wish to sail, there is a name for that heading. These names relate to the angle the wind hits your vessel, and each has its own distinct personality and characteristics due to wind factors. Words like broad reach, beam reach, close reach, close haul, and running are quite intuitive and will soon become part of your nautical lingo.

Below is a diagram depicting the "Points of Sail" of a sailboat. Study and enjoy it and you will see how truly simple it is, except for learning a few new terms. The number is the degree angle the boat is sailing off the wind.

Also note that sometimes some sailors will refer to a close haul as a "beat." It probably originates from the Point of Sail where you will feel the most beat up. In a close haul, you're heading relatively into the wind and the waves.

Scan the code at right and watch this video of a sailboat as it sails around a course.

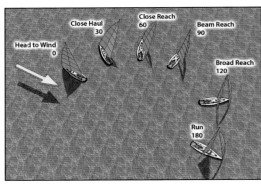

Points of Sail.

The animation below helps you see what the wind vane is doing and how the sail should be set for each Point of Sail. Click on any and all of the Points of Sail and you will see what is happening. Start with Close Haul on starboard.

Head-to-Wind

Head-to-wind means your boat is headed directly into wind. The sails are "luffing" or "flogging" back and forth, and the jib sheets are whipping dangerously. The boat is not moving and you're basically stuck. It's called "stuck in irons."

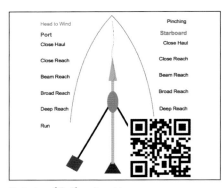

Points of Sail animation.

To get out of "irons," tighten up on the head-sail sheet to one side. Turn the rudder so that the tiller is parallel to the headsail. Since the boat will begin to go backwards slightly, both the sail and rudder act in unison to turn the boat. In the image to the left, the boat will turn clockwise.

Pinching

You might be sort of sailing, but not really. The angle is too close to the wind to create any sail shape. Your speed will be extremely slow and the sails are lightly luffing. The front of the sail is collapsed in on itself and is considered "back winded."

Getting out of irons.

To get out of this, bear away from the wind until the wind vane arrow tail matches one of the stationary tails.

Close Hauled

Close hauled means the wind is as close to the bow as possible while still being able to provide efficient sail power, about 30-45 degrees off the bow.

Close haul.

- The sails are sheeted in as tight as possible.
- Boom is positioned at about the vessel's centerline.
- Headsail should not touch the spreaders.
- As the vessel heels, there is slight weather helm on the tiller, you feel lots of wind in your face.
- Telltales are streaming back.
- (more on weather helm and Telltales soon)

Close Reach

With close reach, the wind is a bit farther back than close haul, somewhere between 50 to 75 degrees off the bow.

Close reach.

- The sails are eased more than closehauled.
- Main boom is off centerline and the headsail is not as tight.
- The vessel heels but not excessively.
- Telltales streaming smoothly.

Beam Reach

On a beam reach, the wind angle is approximately 90 degrees off the bow. It is a very efficient Point of Sail.

- The sails are eased.
- The main boom extends over the side of the vessel. The spreaders may just begin to indent the mainsail. This should be monitored carefully to prevent chafing.

- The boom vang is tightened while the traveler is eased to leeward to deepen the draft of the mainsail.
- The headsail flies full, telltales will stream back with proper sail trim.

Many sailors tend to oversheet the main on a beam reach: let it out. Oversheet means you have pulled in the sheet too far for an efficient set of sail.

On a beam reach, the vessel is relatively flat, it no longer heels, and has excellent speed. You may not feel the wind because it is no longer directly in your face as you look forward.

Beam reach.

Broad Reach and Deep Reach

On a broad reach, the wind angle is 120 degrees off the bow. On a deep reach, the wind angle is 150 degrees off the bow.

At anything more than about 140 degrees off the wind, you are being pushed by the wind. You no longer have lift to contend with, so the telltales are not going to give you much information.

- The traveler is eased down to leeward, increasing the angle of the main.
- At this position, the vessel is simply being pushed by the wind.
- Here is an opportunity to use lots of sail area. But not excessively.
- The luff of the headsail may curl forward of the vessel's forestay.
- The broad reach and deep reach are very comfortable points of sail, but be aware of quick wind shifts.

There are many special sails available to capture more wind, the most noticeable being the spinnaker. These huge, colorful, and billowy sails capture wind for fast sailing.

The sailboat does not heel as it sails with the wind and seas on a broad reach. This is the traditional Point of Sail used by sailors sailing long distances in the trade winds.

To the right, a furling gennaker is used as the head sail while the jib is furled (rolled in

Broad and deep reach.

around the forestay). The gennaker is a larger sail used for sailing in downwind angles.

Running Downwind

The final Point of Sail is when the wind is directly behind the sailboat. This is called running downwind. Now the mainsail totally blankets the headsail. The mainsail can be let out to its maximum, but be aware of spreader interference.

Running downwind.

On this heading, there is no lift on the sails. The headsail can now be positioned on the opposite side of the main. This configuration is called "wing and wing." Sometimes a "whisker pole" is used to hold the headsail out from the mast. In the image to the right, a "bowsprit" is used to increase the size of the headsail.

Running directly downwind with sails positioned on opposite sides can be a little dangerous because without constant attention, the mainsail and thus the VERY HARD boom can gybe across and injure a crew member. Besides this, there is not too much advantage to heading directly downwind even if your destination is downwind. You'll find that gaining some apparent wind by coming back up to 140 degrees gives extra boat speed, which overaccounts for the change in direction and the need to gybe back and forth to maintain an overall direct downwind progression. For this reason, you seldom see a professional sailing downwind.

Wind: Velocity and Direction

Velocity

A sailboat moves through the water because of the pressure the wind projects against your sails. It's imperative that you understand this pressure because it can overpower your sails and your rigging, causing catastrophic damage. Pressure from the wind creates the force on your sails. The mathematical formula is Force = Pressure x Area. So the greater the area of the sails presented to the wind, the more the force on the rig and the boat. Halve the sail area and you halve the force; this is the basis of reefing in high winds, which will be discussed in the following pages.

While it's good to understand the linear relationship between pressure, force, and sail area, there is a far more imperative mathematical formula you must understand. Pressure = 1/2 air density x velocity^2. Since air density is a constant given the conditions, it means that if you double the velocity, the pressure and thus force goes up by 4 times. Or more dramatically, if you go from 4 knots of wind speed to 16 knots, the force goes up 16 times. Or even more dramatically, if you go from 4 knots to 32 knots, the force goes up 64 times.

Given this, you can understand the issues of sailing on a windy, gusty day before you are properly experienced. If you're not prepared or do not know exactly and instantly what to do, a sudden gust can knock you over and break a lot of things.

Wind Directions and Angles

A wind direction when expressed relative to the compass is called the wind direction. When wind direction is expressed relative to the boat, it is called a wind angle. For example, the wind direction is out of the north and the wind angle is 30 degrees off the port bow. This seems like a minor language point, but accurate communication on a sailboat is important.

It's also important to distinguish between apparent wind and true wind. Here is a small recap of this topic more fully covered in the FREE Basic Sail Trim course. (If you have not taken this FREE Basic Sail Trim course yet, now is a good time to take it. Everything makes more sense, and it is a prerequisite to receiving a passing grade for this course.)

True Wind

True wind is the direction the wind is indeed blowing on the planet, as witnessed by flags, smoke, trees bending, etc. If your vessel were standing still, at anchor, or securely in the slip, you would measure true wind speed and direction.

The weather report will tell you the true wind speed and direction (at least it tries to).

However, as we know, true wind is always fluctuating depending upon weather conditions, and turbulence of landmasses, tall buildings, cliffs and mountains, among other things. Use true wind speed forecasts as an approximation, but be aware that it can change (shift) dramatically.

Apparent Wind

Apparent wind is the result of the true wind and your boat speed. Here is an explanation that you can easily grasp because it relates to something you experience almost every warm summer's day.

Scan the code below, right, and play with it by sliding the slider to speed up the car. Then read the text below and replay this animation.

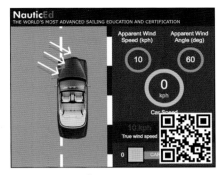

Apparent wind animation.

Put your hand outside the window of your car traveling at 60 miles per hour (100 kph) on a still, warm summer day, and your hand will feel a 60 mph wind coming from the front of the car. That's apparent wind; yet the true wind is zero. What if the car were driving into a 20 mph head wind? Your hand would feel 80 mph. Or if the wind were blowing from behind at 20 mph, your hand would feel 40 mph.

Now, what about a crosswind of 20 mph? Well, we need to do a little Pythagorean Theorem work on this. What is the square root of the sum of 60 squared plus 20 squared? Your hand would feel 63.24 mph and mostly from a direction in front of the car. If the car accelerated to 100 mph, your hand would feel 102 mph, again mostly from the front. If the car decelerates to 10 mph, your hand would feel 22 mph, mostly from the side of the car (and if he car stopped, you'd feel the full true wind of 20 miles per hour from the side of the car). Whatever your hand feels is the apparent wind. The apparent wind equals the true wind when your car is not moving.

When determining direction of the apparent wind, the faster the car goes, the more the apparent wind direction comes from the direction of the travel of the car. Again, imagine the cross wind. At 1 mph forward speed in your car and a 20 mph cross wind, the apparent wind feels almost like the true wind from across the car. As the car accelerates, the wind feels more and more like it is coming from the front.

This is similar to a boat. The faster the boat sails into the wind, the more the apparent wind speed increases and the more it feels like it is coming from the front of the boat.

So now that you understand the difference, let's put the practical application to work for you on a sailboat.

The minute your vessel is no longer standing still, it creates a wind vector of its own, and thus the wind you feel (speed and direction) is altered from the true wind speed and direction. When sailing, apparent wind information is needed for efficient set of the sails, and the information required includes both velocity and direction.

There is fun mathematics associated in determining apparent wind speed, but at this time in your learn to sail quest, you are luckily spared this computational exercise. Sorry. Or perhaps you're glad!

To repeat: the apparent wind speed and direction is the resultant determined by the angle and speed at which the vessel is sailing and the actual true wind speed and angle; it's the wind that you feel on your face, or the back of your neck, that makes you smile when you're out in it.

Apparent wind is also the wind that the boat and the sails feel. Just like your hand feels when it's outside the car. Thus, any telltales on the sails, wind vanes, and wind meters are working with the apparent wind direction and speed. Wind meters with an anemometer will also tell you apparent wind velocity. A wind meter can also tell you the true wind speed and direction from a set of computations that the wind meter does inside its electronics. But again— as you're sailing, you're mostly likely concerned with the apparent wind. True wind knowledge comes in handy when you begin to do navigation, plotting, and course planning.

Imagine 4 sailboats: "A" is stopped and pointed into wind, "B" is heading upwind on a close haul at 30 degrees off the wind, "C" is headed across the wind on a reach, and "D" is headed almost downwind on a broad reach.

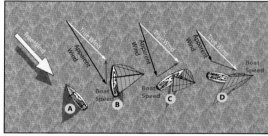

Apparent wind versus Point of Sail.

As you now know, the true wind condition is independent of boat speed or boat direction and remains unchanged for each boat, but the apparent wind varies widely.

"A" is pointed to wind and is therefore stopped. People on "A" feel the wind unaffected by boat speed, and so they feel the true wind.

"B" is more like a car headed into the wind. Thus on an upwind course, the apparent wind is higher and alters in direction to feel like it is coming more from the front of the boat.

Traveling across the wind, "C" would feel the largest change in direction but the smallest change in speed from the true wind. Again, the apparent wind direction feels like it is coming more from the front of the sailboat.

"D" feels a reduction in apparent wind speed. Think about a car driving downwind at 20 mph with a tailing wind at 20 mph. You'd feel nothing. However, "D" also feels the direction of the apparent wind coming more from the front of the boat than the true wind.

Thus people on A, B, C, and D feel completely different wind speeds and velocities, even though the "true wind" is unchanged. In "D," imagine the boat going a lot faster—the "apparent wind" vector would get much shorter and swing more to the front of the boat.

As a general rule of thumb, when on a boat, if you point toward where you feel the wind is coming from (the apparent wind), then move your finger 15 to 20 degrees toward the stern of the boat, that is where the true wind is coming from. It's more so going across the wind and less so heading into or away from the wind.

Next time you're on a boat with an electronic wind meter, toggle between true wind speed indication and apparent wind speed indication. Except standing still, going dead downwind, or headed directly into the wind, in every case, going from apparent to true, the needle will flick more toward 180 degrees—guaranteed. If you're headed into the wind, the true wind speed will be less; and if you're headed downwind, the true wind speed will be higher.

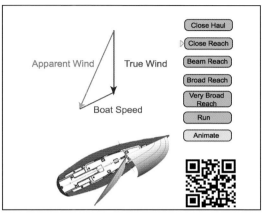

Apparent wind animation.

The code above and to the right is another way to look at it. Tap the buttons to make the boat turn.

Tacking and Gybing Maneuvers

Tacking

When you want to sail in a direction exactly where the wind is coming from—guess what—you can't! The best we can do is to follow a zigzag course by sailing at about 30 to 40 degrees off the wind on one side for some distance, then turning the boat to sail 30 to 40 degrees off the wind on the other side. Then repeat as necessary. Each time we turn so that the bow goes through the point where the wind comes from is called tacking. After the tack, since the wind is on the other side of the boat, the sails must also change sides of the boat.

Tacking is usually performed when you are sailing at angles into the wind, i.e., a beam reach up to a close haul. If you feel the wind on your face, you will probably tack. This means turning the boat toward the wind, through the point of where the wind is coming from and then back downwind a little so that now it is hitting you on the other side of the face/boat.

Gybing

When you want to sail in a direction exactly where the wind is going to—guess what—you can! But ... it has its difficulties because the sails must be held on opposite sides of the boat lest the mainsail "shadow" the headsail from the wind. They are thus balanced somewhat tenuously. Often the headsail is lowered and a spinnaker or gennaker is deployed. We've all seen the gorgeous site of the big, colorful, and sometimes fun sail blowing out over the front of a boat as the boat sails downwind. These sails are either a gennaker or a spinnaker sail used exclusively for sailing in downwind directions.

Sailing downwind.

Usually, however, smart tacticians do not sail directly downwind even if that is the direction of their destination. From the Sail Trim course, you understood that the boat and thus the sails feel only the apparent wind. A smart tactician usually will "crack" off the downwind course a little and aim up at about 140 degrees maximum angle sailing downwind. By doing this, the boat picks up more apparent wind and thus boat speed than what it loses in angle when sailing directly downwind. Similar to tacking, the skipper must zigzag the boat from one tack to another. But this time, since the maneuver means the boat is aiming downwind and the aft of the boat transverses the wind, the maneuver is called a gybe. Some people call it a jibe. Either way is correct. For consistency we will use gybe.

Gybing is usually performed when you are sailing at an angle away from the wind, i.e., a beam reach to a run. If you feel the wind on the back of your neck or around to the side of your face, you will probably gybe the boat. This means turning the boat further downwind, through the point where the wind is blowing to and then around back up a little so that now the wind is hitting you on the other side of the boat.

Tacking and Gybing Maneuvers

The diagram on page 99 shows a typical race course whereby the skipper must expertly maneuver the boat around the course. Careful study of this diagram will reveal all the secrets of sailing in one go. Notice the tacking and gybing maneuvers where the sails shift sides.

Scan the codes below, right, to observe the distinctions between gybing and tacking.

Which maneuver you perform, tacking or gybing, depends entirely on circumstances. Select carefully. Gybing has more potential for accidents, including equipment failures.

To perform either of these maneuvers efficiently, you will need to practice and get the "feel" of your vessel and establish rapport with it.

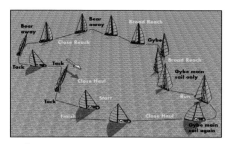

Sailing maneuvers.

How to Tack the Boat

Alert the crew and passengers to this maneuver by announcing, "Prepare to tack," or "Prepare to come about." The crew begins by wrapping the nonworking jib sheet (i.e., upwind sheet, also called the lazy sheet) 2 to 3 times clockwise around the upwind winch drum in preparation for it to become the working jib sheet. Check to ensure the lazy sheet is ready to run clear.

The helmsperson then asks, "Ready?" When the crew replies with "Ready," the helmsman begins turning the vessel's bow through the wind. There are a variety of nautical commands that may be issued, the most common of which is "coming about," but also heard are "helm's alee," "hard alee," "tacking," "helm's over," or "lee ho." All are in vogue as you move the tiller or the wheel as the case may be. The key is to have all the crew understand what is happening.

At the moment the headsail begins to fold in on itself at the forestay, the crew should ease the taut "working" headsail sheet followed by unwinding it from the winch and then allowing the headsail sheet to completely run free. Watch and make sure this sheet does not catch on anything like mast cleats or hatches.

As the headsail comes across the vessel's foredeck, a crew member begins taking up slack on the other headsail sheet, previously prepared and wrapped loosely around the winch. Speed is of the essence here. The faster that crew member brings in the slack, the less the crew member will have to use the winch to tighten the sheet when the load comes on. For this reason, it is a good idea for the helmsperson to make the tack slow. Time spent tightening the sheet by the crew is time lost.

Trim both sails for the new Point of Sail, starting with the headsail first, because the headsail controls the flow of wind (slot effect) over the mainsail. If you are tacking from one close haul to the other, then there is little need to trim the mainsail. Concentrate instead on the jib.

An aside—when tacking, the vessel's bow should be turned through the wind, fast enough to maintain forward momentum.

- If the rudder is turned too quickly, it will act as a brake and the boat may stall in low winds.
- Pulling the tiller over too quickly creates eddies in the water—not too much problem, but it is energy you are taking out of the boat and giving to the water. Best leave the energy (= speed) in the boat.
- Pulling the tiller over too quickly gives the crew no time to properly get the headsail trimmed before the load comes on. This slows the boat.
- If the vessel is turned too slowly, the bow will not come through the wind. In this case, you may get stuck in irons or simply stall. You will need to turn back downwind, gain some speed, and try again.

Safety concerns: The jib sheets whip quite violently with the sail as the boat is pointing head to wind. The new working sheet must be tightened in as fast as possible to minimize the whipping effect. Anyone standing in the way of these whipping sheets can be severely hurt. They can be whipping at over 100 miles per hour (160 km/hr).

How to Gybe the Boat

One of the things that new sailors find slightly intimidating is the act of gybing. Gybing is the act of changing sailing directions when you're sailing downwind so that the stern of the sailboat passes through the wind and one or more sails change sides. This is the functional opposite of tacking, where the bow of the sailboat turns through the wind.

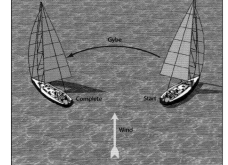

The gybe.

During the gybe procedure, the sails are switched to the other side of the sailboat automatically by the wind.

Gybing is easy and safe—when proper precautions are taken. However, potential problems can arise if the boom is permitted to swing rapidly and unrestrained from one side of the vessel to the other. This can be dangerous to personnel and the vessel, so do it carefully.

The boom swinging across can happen violently when gybing because the wind is blowing from the back end of the mainsail, and once it gets on the other side of the mainsail, the boom swings across fast. During a tack, the wind blows from the leading edge and so this tends not to happen. A chicken gybe discussed soon is actually tacking instead of gybing to avoid the potential dangers of gybing when high winds exist.

To help visualize the dangers of gybing, imagine you are a mast and you attach a piece of plywood to your back so that it extends away perpendicular to your back. Now go outside on a really windy day. Imagine what happens as you turn your face through the point of origin of the wind. Nothing too violent, as the plywood is being blown downwind through the turn. That's a tack. Now keep turning around so that your back goes through the wind. When the wind catches the other side of the plywood, you'll probably be launched over so hard you'll be glad this is only imagination. That's a gybe! Ouch!

On top of all that, since you're probably flying a headsail, as well, you've got to deal with that at the same time. Left unattended during a gybe or done wrong, the headsail will first fly forward, then come around on the wrong side (the downwind side) of the forestay. This makes it a real problem trying to recover it into a sailing position as the boat straightens out on the other side of the wind. And for a new sailor trying to impress their crew, it's totally embarrassing.

So here are the tricks to gybing that make it simple and easy on your sailboat rigging and crew:

1. Begin by alerting crew and announcing: "Prepare to gybe."
2. Ensure loose items below decks are stowed and drinks and gear above decks are secured.
3. Check all around for traffic.
4. Ensure no crew is in harm's way of the boom swinging or lines changing over on the foredeck.
5. Prepare the headsail by hauling in taught on the lazy headsail sheet (the upwind sheet that is not doing anything) and cleating it off around the winch. This will prevent the headsail from wrapping around the forestay during the maneuver, and it will place the sheet almost in position for fine-tuning after the gybe maneuver is complete.
6. Prepare the mainsail by hauling in on the mainsheet, bringing the mainsail toward the center of the sailboat. This will be relatively hard, as there is a lot of pressure on the mainsheet. As you become better at the gybe maneuver

and your crew becomes more finely tuned, you can begin turning the vessel and simultaneously hauling in the mainsheet until it is amidships. Turning reduces the pressure on the mainsail and makes it easier to haul it. But take note that timing has to be perfect. So, until you and your crew are finely honed at gybing, the best practice is to pull in the mainsail before you execute the turn.

Bringing the mainsail close into the center of the sailboat prevents the boom from swinging through a large arc. This, in turn, prevents the boom from building up a great speed as it swings across. It's the speed of the swing that causes the damage on rig and crew.

Of biggest concern is the crew. If the boom is allowed to swing dangerously across at speed, crew can be hit in the head, and quite possibly killed—it has happened. Many crew have been slung overboard and drowned while unconscious. Take heed!

Of second concern is SERIOUS damage to the gooseneck and other parts of the rig. The gooseneck is the connection point of the boom to the mast.

7. The next trick is vital. Otherwise, your sailboat will be violently heeled over and rounded up into the wind. As the boom flips across because the wind is now on the other side, QUICKLY ease the mainsail out to its desired position. If the mainsail is not eased fast enough, the center of pressure of the wind is aft on the rig as the boat completes the gybe. But aft COP pushes the stern of the boat downwind, which rounds the boat up into the wind. **W^{2}NW^3** (Which Was Not What Was Wanted).

    The best way to do this is appoint a crew member to manage the mainsail. Ensure they have the mainsheet wrapped around a winch (clockwise) with the clutch released or uncleated. As the boom flicks over to the other side, immediately release the mainsheet out in a controlled fashion.

8. As the headsail is coming across, another crew member should now release the old working headsail sheet, completely allowing the new leeward working headsail sheet to take the load.

9. Now you have successfully gybed, and the only matter is for the crew to observe the new heading of the vessel and trim both sails accordingly.

The Accidental Gybe

The accidental gybe happens when the helmsperson is not paying close attention. It is a rookie mistake that can cost dearly with injuries (death) and damage. IT MUST BE AVOIDED.

When sailing directly downwind, a rookie helmsperson takes their eyes off the wind indicator and allows the boat to be positioned so that the wind is coming from the same side on which the mainsail and boom are positioned. This happens via a shift in wind or a slight course change. The wind now gets on the other side of the sail and pushes it over; and it comes over fast, bringing a very hard and head-knocking boom with it.

If you are sailing at any angle close to downwind, you must diligently keep an eye on the wind angle.

Sailing by the Lee

Sailing by the lee is possible and done, BUT it is dangerous because you are extremely close to the accidental gybe position above. Sailing by the Lee means that the wind is coming from behind (you are sailing downwind) and anywhere from 0-30 degrees off to the same side as the mainsail. If the mainsail is let all the way out, the wind will still hold the mainsail out rather than swinging it over. But you are riding on the edge.

Sailing by the lee.

When sailing by the lee, make sure a crew member is assigned to the main sheet and is ready to—at less than a moment's notice—quickly haul in on the main sheet to capture the boom before it SLAMS all the way across. Tell all crew members to keep their eyes up and their heads down.

Scan the code, top right, for a video from Wichard, which manufactures a good device called a Preventer. This product slows down a gybe whether it be by accident or not.

Scan code bottom right for a look at another product that actually stops the gybe.

Care must be taken using this device, however: if the gybe is continued through and if the clutch is not released, there will be a lot of force on the sail/rig and your boat will heel over dangerously. If the clutch is released without control of the mainsheet, the boom will swing violently across. This is not a problem if you have an experienced crew.

Scan the code at right for a great video by *Yacht World* magazine, also on gybe preventers.

When sailing downwind, a good safe rule of thumb is: if moving between the foredeck and the cockpit, walk on the same side where the boom is. In this manner, the boom will only swing away from you if an accidental gybe takes place. It's particularly important to teach your crew this as early as possible. As Skipper, be wary of turning the helm over to an inexperienced helmsperson when the boat is going downwind.

Important safety concerns:

- Be aware of the boom coming across fast
- Be aware of whipping jib sheets
- Tighten the lazy jib sheet prior to the gybe to prevent the jib flying forward and around the forestay
- Let out the mainsheet quickly after the boom comes across to prevent excessive heeling

The Chicken Gybe

In high winds, 15 knots and above, the gybing maneuver is not recommended. Rather, the alternate recommended procedure is the "chicken gybe." This maneuver is essentially a 270-degree tack. Instead of turning the boat downwind, you turn the boat up into the wind and perform a normal tack, then bear away from the wind to the desired point of sail.

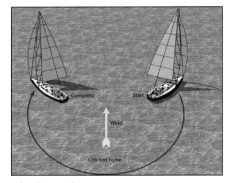

Chicken gybe.

The chicken gybe is mostly performed when the skipper is uncomfortable about the conditions for the gybe, mainly if the wind speed is high.

So, many skippers choose the chicken gybe because it is a much safer maneuver. The end result is the same. You are merely tacking the boat from a broad reach on one side over to a broad reach on the other side. It's simple, easy, effective, and safe. The only thing to watch out for is that the jib sheets will whip back and around quite violently. So, it's a good idea not to have anyone near the jib sheets (i.e., on foredeck).

The following is an animation of the sails as they go through the gybe and chicken gybe maneuvers.

Scan the codes to the right for animations of the boat as it moves through the gybe/chicken gybe maneuvers.

Also in high winds, a gybe maneuver will tend to round the boat up into wind very quickly and cause excessive heeling. This is usually upsetting to the crew. To prevent the excessive heeling, once the mainsail gybes over, you've got to let out the mainsheet as quickly as possible. Getting the mainsheet out will stop the rounding up and heeling over.

Hence, before you go gybing in high winds, become an expert in lower wind conditions first and use the chicken gybe method until you've gained the confidence to gybe correctly every time.

Unfurling or Raising the Sails

You have motored your vessel from the slip into open water and are now ready to unfurl or raise the sails as the sail setup may require. The procedures for deploying the sails are reasonably standardized; however, every sailor will, over time, develop their own routine.

On modern sailboats, mainsails are commonly stored ("stowed") either by being:

- Lowered and lashed onto the boom
- Lowered into a stack pack (a long bag permanently mounted above the boom)
- Rolled into the mast (mast-furled mainsail)
- Rolled onto the boom (boom-furled mainsail)
- Removed and folded into a sailbag for stowage below

There are many opinions as to which is the preferred method, but for now, you will find that each has its pluses and minuses. Sailing is rife with opinions that add greatly to the excitement of this sport.

Sailing is fun!

A Furled Mainsail

If a mainsail is stored rolled up into the core of the mast, it is called a mast-furled mainsail. If it is stored rolled up into the core of the boom, it is called a boom-furled mainsail.

Unfurling: In preparation to unfurl the mainsail, head the vessel into the wind. Depending on wind conditions, you may wish to keep just enough speed, from the engine, to maintain steerage.

The mainsail is unfurled first. Unfurling is done by either raising the sail from out of the boom using the halyard, or hauling the sail from out of the mast using the outhaul.

The following steps provide a guide when the mainsail is furled in the mast:

1. Motor into the wind maintaining steerage
2. Release mainsail furling inhaul line
3. Release tension on the boom vang and mainsheet (very important)
4. Pull (haul) on the outhaul line—this brings the mainsail out of the mast along the boom
5. Tighten the mainsail against the boom by tensing the outhaul line.
6. Trim the mainsail and secure the mainsheet (line - rope)

If the mainsail is to be unfurled from the boom, you first attach the halyard to the "head" of the sail and then raise the mainsail by hauling on the mainsail halyard.

Raising the Mainsail

Many boats these days still do not have an in-mast roller-furling mainsail, and you must therefore raise the sail up the mast by pulling on the main halyard. The luff of the sail will most likely fit into a track and thus will need guiding up. During this process, it's important that the helmsman keep the boat facing directly into the wind. Any side force on the sails will make it very difficult to raise the sail. You can alleviate the force on the mainsail if you are not directly into the wind by further letting out the mainsheet. Care must be taken, however, because

Raise the sails.

the boom will now "flog" (oscillate) from side to side with possible head injury consequences.

The helmsman is also responsible for keeping an eye on traffic and obstacles. It is easy to become distracted by the sail going up.

Just for fun, let's raise the mainsail now.

Once the sail is all the way up, cleat off the halyard and tighten down on the Cunningham if one is available. The amount of tension you put into the leading edge (luff) of the sail via the halyard or Cunningham is proportional to the wind of the day. Light winds require slight tension to keep the sail baggy and give it plenty of shape. High winds require high tension to reduce the curvature of the sail.

The outhaul is another line to help make the sail more efficient. The outhaul is the line that is attached to the clew (bottom aft connection point) of the sail. When you tighten this, it flattens the sail against the boom. On high windy days, you want to tighten the outhaul as much as possible to keep the sail flat thereby reducing the curvature and lift. Don't worry about losing curvature, you already have an abundance of lift from the high wind; at this stage you want to get rid of lift to reduce the heeling of the boat.

In low wind conditions, loosen the outhaul to make the sail baggier and curvier, thereby increasing the lift.

Halyard tension and outhaul adjustments also apply to in-mast roller-furled mainsails.

Turning Off the Engine

Before you switch off the engine, bear away from the wind and get the boat sailing so you have maneuverability. Once you are sailing you may turn off the engine. If the boat is heeling and the lower unit of the engine is out of the water, turn it off fast to prevent overheating from lack of cooling water.

Sailing at last! Is this real freedom or what? You are no longer simply a ground-pounder.

Setting a Course

Next, decide where you want to go. Select a heading (destination), such as a compass heading, a scenic spot in the bay, a distant idyllic island, or maybe a channel marker. When this decision has been made, you will next unfurl/raise the headsail (jib or genoa).

Unfurling the Headsail

Before starting to unfurl the headsail, it is best to have the downwind jib sheet wrapped around the winch 2 to 3 turns (wraps). If the wind is strong, you may wish to head higher into the wind as the jib unfurls, to help control its unfurling motion.

It is time to unfurl the headsail (jib or genoa). With your vessel headed windward, but not directly into the wind, the jib sail is easily unfurled.

Make certain the jib furling line is laid out so that it can flow out without tangling. Now you simply pull (haul) on the downwind jib sheet to shape the headsail. As the headsail begins to fill with wind, it may unfurl rapidly by itself.

Care must be taken: more than often, the furling line will tangle. The crew member hauling on the jib sheet to tension and shape the headsail must monitor that this tangle does not happen. Otherwise, he/she can damage the furling system. Additionally, as the furling line goes out, very slight back tension will prevent the furling line from overwrapping in the furling drum. An overwrap can be disastrous because it is very difficult to fix.

Furling the Headsail

You'll find that if you head the boat in a downwind direction, furling the headsail will be much (much) easier. To furl the headsail, have one crew member slowly release the jib sheet while another crew member hauls in on the furling inhaul. Slight tension should be kept on the jib sheet so that the headsail rolls reasonably tight around the forestay. Often enough tension can be created by having the jib sheet wrap once around a winch as you pull in on the furling line.

If possible, steer the boat to a deep broad reach point of sail when furling. This makes the furling operation so much easier.

Care must be taken: The crew member hauling the furling line must monitor the amount of line remaining in the furling drum. Otherwise, the end of the furling line in the drum can be reached and continuous hauling can cause damage. For this reason, it is a bad idea to use a winch on the furling line.

In some circumstances, you'll need to drop a furling type headsail. This is simple, as the luff of the sail usually contains a boltrope which slides up into a track on a plastic extrusion, which is slid over the forestay. The sail will need to be unfurled. Simply release the headsail halyard and pull down on the leech of the sail. To raise the headsail back up again, just guide the bolt rope into the track in the forestay extrusion and tension the halyard.

Raising the Headsail

It is common for boats to have neither a roller-furling mainsail nor roller-furling headsail. In this case, you'll be raising the headsail up the forestay. The headsail is usually stowed neatly in a bag below decks. Depending on the wind you'll want to select the appropriate size headsail. High winds dictate a smaller sail; low winds require a bigger sail.

The luff of a headsail often has "hanks." These are small clips that clip around the forestay. Prior to leaving the marina, you will want to prepare the headsail for deployment. First, you'll need to lay the headsail out on the foredeck. You'll then need to attach the headsail halyard to the head (top connection point) of the headsail, the tack of the headsail to a clip mounted at the base of the forestay, and then the clew of the headsail to the jib sheets. Run the jib sheets back through the appropriate fairleads that guide the jib sheets back to the cockpit. You'll need to be versed on the bowline knot, as this is the recommended knot for the jib sheet to attach to the clew. Now clip the hanks onto the forestay. Use sail ties to tie the sail down to the foredeck so that it is secure until you want to raise the sail once you are out in the bay.

After you have deployed the mainsail and the boat is sailing, untie the sail ties as another crew member pulls on the headsail halyard. Once this is complete, it is advisable to move back to the cockpit, as the flapping headsail and jib sheets can be very dangerous in high winds.

Finally, tighten up on the headsail sheet. There you have it, you're now fully under sail.

After the jib is fully unfurled or raised, use the winch to further haul (pull) in the jib sheet to establish the desired jib sail trim. The tension necessary for the most efficient sail plan depends on the cut of the jib sail, wind speed, and vessel heading.

Check how the wind is hitting your vessel and trim both sails for efficiency. It is that simple.

If your desired destination happens to be directly into the wind, you will need to make an adjustment. The one place you are unable to sail is directly into the wind. This wind angle is the "no-sail zone." The size of this angle varies with vessels, but is approximately 45 degrees off dead on.

The headsail.

Dousing the Headsail

To douse (bring down) the headsail at the end of your sail is also pretty simple. It is best to have the engine on and be heading directly into the wind. Although heading into the wind is not completely necessary, it makes dousing easier.

Just release some tension from the sheets and uncleat the halyard. The sail should drop onto the foredeck. Make sure you use sail ties again to tie the sail to the foredeck or lifelines to stop it from self-deploying.

Sail Trim

Setting the sails to the Point of Sail as discussed will get you really close to a good sail set, but the true finesse in sailing is understanding sail trim.

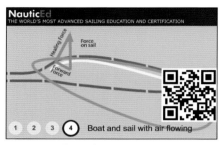

A wing and a sail.

With sail trim knowledge, you use the tell-tails to observe the flow of air over the sails to perfect the sail set and maximize the efficiency. Tell-tails are pieces of ribbon or wool threads where the leading edge is glued to the sail. By observing the flow of the tell-tail, the sail trimmer can visualize the flow of the wind over the sail at that point.

Now is a good time to remind you that if you have not already visited the FREE Basic Sail Trim course online, do so now. There is no better introductory course than the NauticEd FREE Basic Sail Trim course. The course is loaded with animations to help you gain a very practical knowledge base of how to trim the sails.

Just a reminder that a sail is a wing that moves the boat forward. It can't be any other way. If the wind was always just pushing on the sails, how could the wind push the boat in an upwind direction?

Reefing

It is important to realize that excessive heeling is not making you go fast. To the

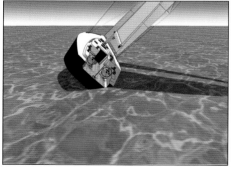

Overheeling.

contrary, you will slow down under such conditions. The image on the bottom of the previous
page shows a boat being excessively heeled over.
It is uncomfortable for the crew, and it puts excessive strain on the rig and makes the boat go slower
because the wind is stalling on the backside of the
sail. To speed up the boat you need to reef the sail.

Reefing of sails should begin at or around
12 to 16 knots of wind. Reefing is simply the art
of reducing the amount of sail area. It reduces
the heeling over force from the wind and helps
the wind stay attached to the leeward side of the
sail, thus reducing turbulent inefficient flow of
wind.

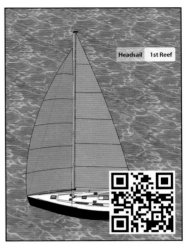

Reefing.

Reefing Roller-Furling Sails

Reefing using roller-furler sails is by far the easiest way of reefing. You simply wind
up the sail until you are satisfied with the sail size. Watch the QR code above for a
basic animation.

In general, for your first reef at about 12 to 16 knots, you should furl up
the sail about 18 inches (45 centimeters). Around 18 to 22 knots, you'll need
another reef; for this second reef, you should furl in the sail another 18 inches
(45 cm). As you gain experience with your boat, you'll get the feel for how
much to reef in. Essentially, if your boat is heeling over a lot, you'll need to reef
in more.

So which sail do you reef first? The headsail or the mainsail? The answer is
pretty complex and involves the design of your boat and rig. Although a full discussion is given in our more advanced Sail Trim course, these are the factors to consider now: When you reef a sail, you are moving the center of pressure point that
the wind acts on the sail relative to the boat. That is, making the triangle smaller
moves the center of that triangle forward on the boat. This affects the dynamic relationship between the rudder, the keel, and the sails.

In a practical sense, then, test out your boat's behavior by reefing the different
sails in different orders on a windy day (with minimal gusts) and feel the changed
pressure on the rudder. As a novice sailor, this is going to be hard. As you gain
more experience, you'll feel the difference. We say all this to ward off the concept
of a formula of which sail to reef first. The process is dynamic. Given all that, if
you are just starting out, primarily all you are trying to do is reduce heeling and

reduce the forces on the rig. So start by reefing the mainsail, then move onto the headsail.

Some mainsail roller furling systems have a ratchet-type lever on the furler. This is used in reefing. It prevents the sail from unwinding after you have just reefed it in.

The illustration to the right shows the mast extrusion and how the sail is rolled up into the mast.

The next illustration shows the Selden roller furler ratchet system. By turning the reefing winch, the sail winds up inside the mast. The endless furling line allows the crew to turn the reefing winch from the cockpit. The ratchet lever will prevent the sail from unwinding. Thus, to unfurl the sail, the ratchet level must be set to "free."

Both illustrations are courtesy of Selden.

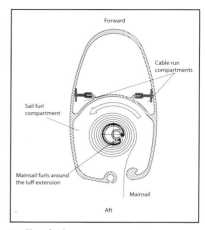

Roller furler mast extrusion.

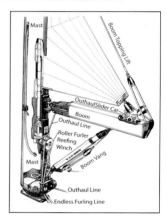

Roller furler system.

Traditional Reefing Systems

Most smaller keelboats do not have a roller-furling mainsail. The mainsail must be hoisted up with the main halyard to begin sailing. When reefing, the mainsail must be lowered to reduce its sail area.

At right is a basic animation. It shows replacing the number 1 headsail with a number 3 headsail that is smaller. (The larger the number the smaller the sail. Why? Just is). It also shows lowering the mainsail to the predetermined reefing points. From the above discussion on which to reef first, the order in the animation is not showing the order of reefing. Like we said above, this depends on the boat and rig.

Reefing animation.

With headsails that are hoisted, as opposed to furling, there is no reefing ability. Rather, you change out the sail for a smaller one.

To Reef the Mainsail:

At the front (luff) of the sail there are usually two reefing points, the first and second (aka primary and the secondary). The primary is the first reef you'll put in for wind speeds of approximately 12 to 16 knots. The secondary reef will need to be put in at about 18 to 22 knots.

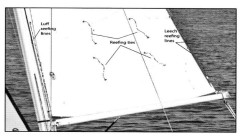

Here is the procedure:

Reefing ties.

1. Decide if you are going to use the primary or secondary reefing points
2. Check the boom topping lift so that when you ease the halyard down, the boom does not drop completely into the cockpit
3. Ease the mainsheet so that there is no load on the sail from the wind
4. Ease the main halyard
5. Ensure the Cunningham hook is into the appropriate reefing point and tighten so that the reefing point is brought down to the boom level (lowering the sail)
6. The halyard must then be tightened followed by final tensioning of the Cunningham
7. At the leech of the sail, the corresponding reefing must also take place

The leech reefing lines may be secured at the aft of the boom or they may run down to the boom, travel forward inside the boom, down the mast and back along the deck through a series of pad eyes to the cockpit. Pulling in on the appropriate reefing line will lower and thus reef the leech of the sail.

A convenient setup on some reefing systems is a single line reefing system. With a single line reefing system, one line acts to pull down both the luff and leech of the sail simultaneously. Here is a video from Selden Masts showing a single line reefing system. If you have one installed on your boat, you will love how easy it is to reef.

Whenever you are reefing the mainsail, observe the boom topping lift line and the main sheet and ensure that they are not tight; otherwise, these will interfere with your ability to tighten the leech reefing lines.

The holes in the sail at the reefing points are called cringles. In some cases, there are additional cringles in the center of the sail between each reefing point. Small reefing tie lines go through these cringles to secure the sail to the boom when it is reefed.

"Shaking out the Reef"

Releasing the reefing lines and raising the sail back up fully is called shaking out the reef. Here's how to do this:

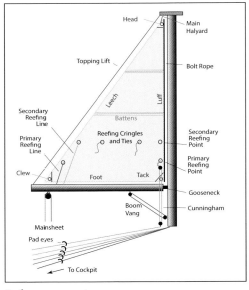

Sail components.

1. Ease the mainsheet
2. Undo any reefing ties in the center of the sail
3. Ease the Cunningham completely
4. Ease the leech reefing lines
5. Raise the mainsail halyard
6. Trim the mainsail
7. Check that topping lift is loose.

The above illustration shows many of the components of the sail and the traditional reefing system.

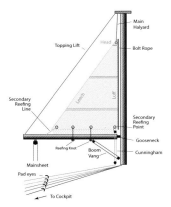

Sail reefed.

The illustration to the left shows the same sail reefed to the secondary reefing position.

When reefing, you do one sail at a time. You can reef the boat while still under sail, with the other sail still propelling the boat. A close haul is best. Heading to wind is an option, but all the sails begin to flap wildly, which can be dangerous because of the whipping sheets.

In heavy weather, reefing usually means someone going forward of the cockpit. Ensure this person is harnessed to the jacklines, the lines connected to the deck running the length of the boat.

When going sailing, prior to heading out of the marina, ascertain if reefing will be possibly necessary. If so, prepare the boat for reefing prior to leaving the still waters of the marina. Use the weather forecast rather than trying to determine the wind speed from the water in the marina. That is a bad gauge because of the protection from the breakwaters.

Heave To

What is Heave To?

When you have successfully hove to (heaved to), your sailboat will be in a stable situation with the mainsail and headsail still up. Your forward speed will be minimal and you'll be sliding downwind slightly. This makes it an ideal strategy for the following situations:

- Lunch, simply taking a rest, or instructor debriefing
- Storm tactics and reefing
- Conditions are too rough and you need a break
- Man overboard recovery
- Boarding by another vessel (i.e., crew change during a race, or law enforcement safety inspection)

Essentially you're under full sail but nearly stopped! Cool, eh?

How to Heave To and its Mechanics

The books say that to heave to, you tack the boat and leave the headsail cleated to windward and the tiller all the way to leeward (wheel to windward). While that is technically correct, there are a lot more things to consider and understand in order to correctly heave to.

The mechanics of the heave to situation are that the forward speed of the boat has dropped to a minimum because the headsail is backwinded and the mainsail has been eased out far enough to reduce nearly all of the forward driving lift on the sail. The backwinded headsail creates a large turning moment on the boat to turn it downwind. However, as the boat turns downwind, it tends to pick up a little speed. As the boat picks up a little speed, the windward locked wheel causes the rudder to turn the boat back upwind, killing off the speed. It creates a little seesaw action. You can adjust the seesaw action by adjusting the set of the headsail, the mainsail, and the rudder angle. Each boat will seesaw a little differently in differing wind conditions and due to the distances of the rudder and the headsail center of pressure positions around the hydrodynamic pivot point of the vessel. Once the boat is settled, by making small adjustments to the angle of the rudder, the amount the mainsail is eased, and by the "depth" or flatness of the headsail, a skilled operator can make very useful adjustments to the exact way in which the boat is lying to the wind and seas. Practice practice practice! When that storm comes, you'll be glad.

Watch the animations to the right and hit pause throughout to read the explanations.

While the animation period is about 12 seconds, in real life it is 30 seconds to 1 minute.

Heave to Animation.

A Cool Trick about Heaving To!

The first thing to think about is (if you can) lie in a heave-to position so that your boom is on the port side. Why? So that you're technically sailing "on starboard tack," putting you in a more advantageous stand-on position with regard to the Navigation Rules vis-a-vis other sailboats "on port" tack. Wouldn't want to disturb our lunch, now would we? It's not a big deal but just something most people may not have considered.

How to Heave To

Once you've got the heave to mastered, you'll enjoy having this little skill under your belt. But you've got to practice it a few times. To enter into a hove-to position, if practical, start out on a on a port tack with the headsail sheeted in tight. Tack the boat slowly onto a starboard tack (bleeding off some speed while head-to-wind), but leave the headsail cleated (i.e., don't tack the headsail). Turn the boat so that you're on a close reach (60 degrees off the wind) and let out the mainsail most of the way out so that it is luffing. Now wait until the rest of the boat's headway speed bleeds off. That's the key part. If you turn the rudder to windward (the wheel to windward or the tiller to leeward) before the speed bleeds

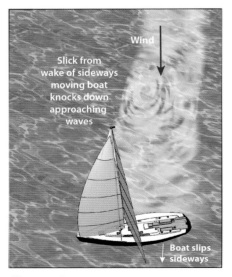

Heave to in a storm.

off, the momentum of the boat may carry it through another tack. Once the speed has bled off, turn the rudder all the way to windward (wheel to windward or tiller to leeward) and lock it in that position (lashing the tiller).

Heaving To in a Storm

It's really important to realize that heaving to in a storm is very wise. With one huge caveat: since you slowly slide sideways through the water, make sure you have plenty of sea-room distance to leeward to avoid rocks, shoals, or the other hard stuff (like land!). Heaving to in a storm gives you and your crew a rest from the elements. And it can be a safer means of riding out a storm rather than trying to sail it out. In a heave to position, the boat is in a completely stable position. You should probably lower or deeply reef the main or raise a storm trisail (very small mainsail) as well as a small headsail to reduce loads on the rig. Here's the kicker that is really cool – since the boat will be slipping sideways, a wake is left to windward. Any breaking waves hit this "slick" and flatten out, thus reducing the wave action on your vessel. Now that's really cool.

A Heave To Trick

When you're settled down into the heave-to position and everything is balanced, use a preventer line to "prevent" the boom slapping around wildly with sudden variable gusts, save wear on the rig, prevent an accidental gybe, or worse yet a bonk on the head if you need to go forward.

Using Heave To in a Man Overboard Situation

Heaving to can be a very effective crew overboard recovery technique. The very moment the victim goes over the side, you can crash tack the boat and go into a heave-to position. You must be sure that the victim is able to swim and that they did not sustain injury while falling. Heaving to in a man overboard situation isn't a technique often taught and therefore isn't considered in the panic of the situation. It's your decision whether to heave to or not in this situation, but it will keep you from getting too far away from your friend in the water, which is clearly the biggest danger.

Ultimately, in a man overboard situation, we recommend getting the engine on and the sails down. The biggest danger from turning on the engines is not chopping your friend up—you're smart enough not to do that—it's getting a line wrapped around the prop in all the panic and then not having the maneuverability. So just make that part of your "engines-on" routine in crew overboard practice. Next time you're out, practice man (or woman) overboard.

But we digress. Back to heave to: So there you have it, you're now a heave to expert. NOT! You haven't practiced it enough yet! And while you're out there practicing it, have fun.

Exiting a Heave-to Position

Exiting a heave-to position is simple!

1. Release the jib sheet, straighten the tiller, and haul in on the main sheet. OR
2. Gybe out of heave to by turning the tiller to the other side and gybing the mainsail. Use normal gybe precautions.

Depth and speed meter.

Instruments

Key Instruments

One of the key instruments you will constantly use is your depth and speed meter. Pictured above right is a typical device.

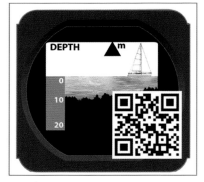

It shows that the depth of the water is 9.8 feet and the speed of the boat through the water is 6.35 knots. Care must be taken to understand from where the depth is measured. Is it the water surface or is it the depth below the keel? If your keel is 5 ft (1.7m) deep, then your boat will hit bottom when the meter is still reading 5 ft (1.7m) if the meter was set up to read from the surface. Most devices have the ability to offset the depth based on the keel depth. It is also wise to add in another 5 ft (2 m) of safety factor.

Depth animation.

Devices can get quite sophisticated and can show a bottom contour, much the same as the one above. The arrow will show you if the depth is increasing or decreasing.

The speed measurement typically comes from an impeller that spins because of the passing water velocity. If you are operating in current flow conditions from tides or river flow, the speed indicated is through the water not relative to the land. In some cases, then, you might think you're going 6.35 knots, but actually, you could be moving backwards in the extreme case. Additionally, the impeller can become clogged with algae, which affects the measurement. You should check and clean your impeller often.

Another key instrument used on larger sailboats is a wind meter that replaces the wind vane at the top of the mast. For now, we'll stick with the wind vane teaching and leave the wind meter for the big boat skipper course.

GPS and navigation instruments will be covered later in the Chapter 8.

Helpful Hints about Wind

Since the existence of wind is the primary reason we can sail, it is prudent to know all we can about it. Here are a few helpful tips:

- 1/2-second glances ONLY at the wind vane at the top of the mast
- Less technical signs of wind direction and velocity include flags, tell-tails, your hair, and birds. Birds, when given the opportunity, generally sit with their beak into the wind.
- Ripples on the water form 90 degrees to the wind
- If you put your nose directly into the wind, you will hear the wind equally in both ears. That is, unless you have hearing problems.

Trimming the sails.

There are many ways to judge how the wind is hitting your vessel, and these tend to become intuitive with experience—you simply sense the wind. This is when you truly have the "feeling" of sailing.

Take note when the boat heels over or stands up.

At a sailing group meeting, someone mentioned she was having trouble determining if the boat was pinching or not. Pinching is a term to describe the boat heading too close to the wind. Someone is usually doing this if they are trying to sail to a destination that is too close to where the wind is coming from. When you do this, your boat speed reduces dramatically and you're better off bearing away from your destination, picking up speed, and tacking one last time to your destination.

When you start pinching, the apparent wind will be less than 30 degrees off the bow of the boat. It means you're heading too close to the origin of the wind and that the wind cannot provide lift and pressure properly on the sails. With no pressure, the heeling force is reduced and so the boat literally "stands up" straight. So the scenario is that you're sailing along, heeling over, and you begin to feel the boat stand up straight. It's a good indication that you're starting to pinch and you'll need to bear away.

Scan the code to the right.

The concept of increased wind speed and changing course will potentially bamboozle you when starting out. From the NauticEd FREE Basic Sail Trim course, you gained a better understanding of true and apparent wind than most sailors on the planet. You know that if either the boat speed or true wind speed changes in magnitude, this affects the direction and speed of the apparent wind. This creates the need to make course corrections.

Some wind shift definitions:

- Wind shifting forward will mean the wind that you feel comes now more from the front of the boat.
- Wind shifting aft will mean that the wind that you feel comes now more from the stern.
- Wind veering will mean wind changes in a clockwise direction, that is, if it was a northeaster, then a veered wind might be an easterly.
- Wind backing means wind changes in a counterclockwise direction, that is, if it was a northeaster, then a backed wind might be a northerly.

You can almost instantly tell what the true wind is doing by the action of the boat. If the boat suddenly stands up taller (less heeling), the true wind has gotten lighter or has shifted forward—thus, you should bear away. If the boat heels farther over, the true wind has gotten stronger or has shifted aft—thus, you should head up.

Actions when on upwind headings:

- true wind gets lighter—boat stands up—bear away
- true wind shifts forward—boat stands up—bear away
- true wind gets stronger—boat heels over—head up
- true wind shifts aft—boat heels over—head up

Holding a Straight Course

Let me slightly digress for a bit here with an article I had published that puts the spotlight on what I think is an essential skill for all sailors.

Holding a straight course is an imperative skill to master as you learn to sail. As an experienced sailor, nothing is more distracting to a good day out sailing than a novice helmsperson swinging the boat in all directions. What I've found is that often a new sailor has been taught to "fly the tell-tails" too early in the learn-to-sail process. Tell-tails are short pieces of ribbon mounted on the sails. When they fly backwards along the sails, it means that the airflow is flowing smoothly; in turn, this means the sail is set correctly.

It's no question that all sailors are keen to introduce and teach others to sail. What a great community of passionate people. So whether you're a novice sailor learning to sail or an experienced sailor who loves to teach, this will be important.

As a sailing instructor and having owned my own practical sailing school, I have taught many people to sail. I've discovered that teaching to fly the tell-tails too early almost inherently invites the novice to be sailing all over the map. This is because the sailor is spending too much time watching the sails, watching the wind indicator and the wind meter, and not enough time looking out of the sailboat.

The issue really is that there is a delay between a course change and the tell-tails. So the new sailor tends to wait until the tell-tails are flying correctly before looking up and straightening the helm out. But by the time the sailboat is straightened out, the new correct Point of Sail has been overshot. The novice then tries to bring the sailboat back but overshoots again. And thus there is a constant "S" curve of trailing wakes out behind. A good thing to do is to point out the curvy wake to the novice so they can see what they have been doing.

The biggest mistake occurs when adjusting back up wind to a close haul position. If this is over stood, the boat can auto tack over to the other side. An auto tack occurs when the wind catches the headsail on the opposite side, pushing it through the wind and causing an involuntary tack. It's an extremely common occurrence with new sailors and creates a lot of confusion as to why this happens. It also creates a lot of calamity and is a pretty embarrassing thing to do as the helmsperson. And you'll find that you're resorting to saving face by blaming the wind for a big change in direction. LOL. The term is called "the wind clocked" . . . But in reality, the wind doesn't clock. You just over stood the wind and got auto tacked.

So let's fix that, shall we?

Introducing Rule A thru Z, 1 through infinity—**Keep your eyes out of the sailboat.**

When you drive a car and you want to speed up to 50 miles per hour (mph) (80 kph), you don't do the following: Set your car going straight then watch the speedo intently until you reach 50 mph, then look up to make sure everything is ok. No! Instead, you keep your eyes out of the car, watch the road and traffic and make small steering adjustments to stay between the lines. You flick your eyes to the speedo for perhaps 0.5 seconds every 5 seconds or so. When you reach 45 mph, you lift your foot slowly, and if you're a good driver you'll probably land right bang on 50 mph, having stayed between the lines all the way.

Let's bring that concept over to sailing.

What you don't want to do is the following: hold your eyes on the tell-tails (speedo) until they are flying right and then look up. No! What you want to do is keep your eyes out of the sailboat watching your heading and traffic and flick check your eyes to the tell-tails and wind indicators for 0.5 seconds about every 5 seconds or so.

With this simple revelation, you'll never auto tack again and your wake will be straight.

Now, here's how to make adjustments for wind changes. You're sailing along toward a distant hilltop on a distant island and see that you need an adjustment to lee. As you begin to learn to sail better and your experience increases, you'll be able to determine from the tell-tails how much of an adjustment is needed. For now, a 5 degree adjustment is a good starting point. First, make the adjustment with your eyes. Pick a 5 degree change on the hilltop and turn the sailboat toward that new point. Wait until the sailboat straightens out on that new point, then check the tell-tails. If more adjustment is needed, repeat the process. Note that you're not watching the tell-tails. You're just checking them when the boat is heading straight. Using this method, you'll reduce or stop any over standing on the points that you want to sail to.

When teaching this, I always get the question, "Um duh, what if I'm not heading toward an island?" Well, there is always something, and if there's not something, there is a cloud. I doubt very much that you'll be learning this in the middle of the ocean without land in sight. Even if land is not directly ahead, there is land to the side. Make your adjustments according to the relative position of land on a shroud line or something on the boat. The point is that with your eyes out of the boat, you can see your boat turning. Once you're an experienced sailor, you won't have to worry about holding a straight course, it will all be inherent. But for now, get out and learn to sail and learn to hold a straight course.

Just like watching tell-tails of the wind meter, by watching a compass instead of land or a cloud is also not a good idea. Compasses lag like the tell-tails, as do wind meters. Get your eyes out of the sailboat.

So the secret to sailing a straight line is always aiming at something in the distance or having a relative bearing on something in the distance against something on the boat so that your eyes are telling you if you are turning or not. When making adjustments to your heading, keep your eyes out of the sailboat so that they are telling you how much your boat is turning. Make small adjustments according to those distant objects and flick check your eyes for ½ second to the tell-tails or wind meter (or compass if you're turning onto a new compass heading).

Keep your eyes out of the sailboat. And besides, it's safer; you're keeping your eyes out for traffic at the same time.

And if you can't remember "Keep your eyes out of the sailboat," remember this one:

You're a sailor if you can ...

hold a drink

hold a conversation

... and hold a course.

And if you can do that while telling a joke, then you're an advanced sailor.

Practical Suggestions

Remember each vessel, including sails, has a personality reflecting its construction and how it reacts to conditions in which it is sailing.

- The closer to the wind you are sailing, the closer in the sails should be trimmed.
- Let the sails out until each sail just begins to flutter, and then pull them slightly back in. This will give you a perfectly trimmed sail
- There is a saying regarding sail trim: "when in doubt—let it out." This works well because if the sail is luffing—there is no doubt you should pull it in. Thus, only doubt can exist if it is set too tight or just right (see the bullet above)

Sailing regatta.

- When the wind is directly behind the vessel, sails should be out as far as possible. However, in this situation the mainsail will block all the wind from getting to the headsail. One way to counter this is to fly the jib on the other side. This is called sailing wing and wing
- Every Point of Sail has a distinct personality or feeling relative to the vessel
- When the vessel is sailing dead downwind and the sails are set wing and wing, the specific tack defined for give way issues is determined by the side the main boom is set. For example, if the boom is set on the starboard side

it means by definition that the wind is coming from over the port side and therefore the boat is determined to be on port and must therefore give way to vessels "on starboard."

Sail trimming provides physical and mental exercise for the crew, especially in regattas. As sailors gain experience, they add these to their personal bag of skills.

Motor Sailing

When wind and time are issues, you may wish to consider motor sailing. This means you will use your auxiliary engine for propulsion, sometimes in conjunction with your sail(s). When using sails and engine power, be careful not to allow the boat to heel very much, as the water intake may come out of the water, burn out the water impeller, and cause damage to the engine.

If you are sailing directly into the wind when waves or swells are present, sometimes keeping the mainsail up and tightly sheeted will stabilize/reduce the rocking effect of the boat. Certainly, douse the headsail; otherwise, it will flog, luff, flap, and make a lot of noise. Also, flogging sails fatigue the sail and the parts to which they are connected.

Motorsailing.

For purposes of give-way vs. stand-on, you are now a power vessel, even if your sails are up. When your engine is used for propulsion, the sailing vessel under the rules becomes a power vessel.

Rule 25 (e) also applies: *A vessel proceeding under sail when also being propelled by machinery shall exhibit forward where it can best be seen a conical shape, apex downwards.*

Above, the sailing vessel under power and sail is on a starboard tack, correctly displaying the under-power day shape. She must give-way to the port tack sailing vessel.

This NauticEd chapter on sailing techniques is infinite in scope and continually evolving. It is the heart of sailing. You will continually be adding to this lexicon as you sail.

Chapter 7
Communications

Nonelectronic Communications

Sailing has been around for thousands of years. Electronic Communication has been around for less than 100 years.

The Slow Old Days

My Dad was a radio operator on a DC-3 during WWII. His stories of communicating using Morse Code were boundless, from gaining landing patterns to communicating emergencies, such as the time their landing gear would not come down or when another plane in the squadron was shot up on a mission. He was a pioneer in a new age of communication. Today we can't even imagine that slow of a data rate. Some of us used to use 14.4 k dial up modems. Arrhhh!

So before the harnessing of electrons and radio waves, humankind used many other forms of communication. Many are still used today.

Forms of nonelectronic communication include:

- Verbal
- Hand signals
- Flags and pennants
- Sound-making devices, bells, horns, sirens, whistles, and cannons
- Megaphones—just an improvement on verbal
- Flares

Each of these forms has unique uses depending on the situation. Yet most all of these require the understanding of their meaning. Even with verbal communication, you have to be careful because of all the terminology.

Verbal Communications

Unfortunately, many a newbie sailor has been turned off sailing by a few crusty captains because of the verbal communication style (aka abuse). Don't be a crusty sailor. Below are a few people skills inserted into this course.

A loud clear voice is often preferred to gain the attention of someone not looking. The most common of these would be to announce "STARBOARD" in a potential sailboat-on-sailboat collision situation. By stating this, you are stating that there is a close quarters situation, that collision is possible, and you are stating you are the Stand-On vessel.

It is your responsibility to state this: the other boat may not have seen you, they may be completely unaware of the rules, or they may believe they might squeak by.

Yelling is out. Loud clear voice is in. We say this because the word yelling has a negative connotation. And creating negative situations only heightens emotions. We are all familiar with road rage, and the truthful person would admit that they, at some time, have been guilty of it even to the slightest degree. If you've ever done the bird—the finger—then you have been suckered into your negative self.

We address yelling and road rage (on the water) here a little more because it's important. Despite the wide expanse of the ocean, there is no room for negativity on the water.

Viktor Frankl, a WWII concentration camp prisoner and renowned psychiatrist, developed the notion of logotherapy, the theory that we try to attach meaning to everything. We attach meaning to someone cutting us off in traffic; we attach meaning to being on the receiving end of the bird; and we attach meaning to being yelled at. In Steven Covey's book *The Seven Habits of Highly Effective People*, he integrates Frankl's notion and adds that we as humans have the ability to see an action, make a decision on how to react, and then perform the reaction. Animals, on the other hand, only have action followed by instant reaction.

As an example, let's assume we get cut off in traffic. We as humans have the ability to think about that, to make a decision about the meaning of that (if we want) and the ability to decide what to do about it. The key word is "ability." It does not necessarily mean that we act upon what we think or decide. Just that we have the ability. What is it about someone cutting us off in traffic? What meaning do we attach to that? Did they do it on purpose? Maybe, maybe not. In most cases, probably not. Even in addressing the case that they did it on purpose, we still have the ability to decide "should I let that person continue with their crappy day or should I teach him a lesson so he'll never do that again in his entire life?" In the decision process, we get to bring in our human selves and decide that we don't have to attach meaning to it; that it might have been a mistake, or that even if it was on purpose, who cares? Why let it ruin my perfect day?

The trick is, Covey states, to practice inserting ourselves into the decision before the instant animal reaction.

On the water, you'll find there are a lot of inexperienced people out there. Novices, newbies, old hats who have not bothered to learn the rules, whoever— they are all out there. However, there is only one reason you are on the water and that is to enjoy yourself. To recreate = re-create. Re-create your good experiences. Don't let others ruin your day. Make a decision to make a decision between the action and your reaction.

Instead of yelling, "*Learn the #@$% rules ya &*&^%*." which, as we all know, is only going to get you the finger in return, you might buy the guy a drink back at the yacht club and say something like, "whew that was a close one out there. I thought I was the stand-on vessel but perhaps I was wrong. What were your thoughts?"

Another way of looking at this all is to put yourself in their shoes. Have you ever made a mistake in traffic? Well, maybe that was you in another body making a mistake. It was a wise man many years ago who said, "Let he who is without sin, cast the first stone." We all make mistakes. Let it go.

The point is to act like Lincoln, who was known as a great leader because of his leadership skills, not because of his title. What are your leadership skills at the yacht club or on a boat? People will follow you on a boat because they think (even unknowingly) that you are a good leader. It's not because you are a self-proclaimed captain; it's not because of your experience. In the corporate world, people go back to work the next day under a bad leader because they have a job to try to keep. On a boat, you will find out your leadership skills pretty quickly by the number of your solo sailing days. In the corporate world, you can expound upon your experience, berate and belittle as much as you want; on a boat, it's back to solo sailing if you behave like this.

We really encourage you to scan the code to the right and read this article on our blog site on how to be a good leader on a sailboat.

Take, for example, the yeller, the skipper who yells at his crew, his spouse, and his friends. This is just a bad leader. "But," the skipper says, "it was necessary, we were about to hit the dock." The best way to hit a dock is to freeze up your crew by yelling at them. If you use an authoritative, clear, loud voice with specific instructions, you will get things done smoothly and perfectly and maintain/increase your respect. For example, "Mike. We are going to hit the dock. Please take this fender now and go up front. Put it between the boat and the dock so we don't crash into it. Thanks."

Back to using a loud clear voice, think about your audience. Can they understand what you are saying using the terminology? Can they even hear you? A classic case where communications are compromised is between the bow and the helmstation; it is near impossible in wind. Hand signals are preferred, although bigger, more sophisticated boats use microphones and ear pieces.

Hand Signals

There are universal signals that work for most people, but it is a good idea to agree upon a set of hand signals that work with your crew.

Important ones:

Using hand signals.

- A closed fist is stop.
- A flat open hand pumping slowly up and down is slow down.
- A flat open hand pushing aft is stop the boat in the water.
- When anchor retrieving, the bow person points to the anchor so that the helmsperson can steer that way.
- A hand with flicking open and closed fingers means ease that line (let out slowly).
- A twirling upward finger means bring in that line.

Scan the code at right and watch this video from our friends at Yachting Education (.com).

Flags and Pennants

Flags and Pennants are not used extensively, except in a few cases. The most important ones to know are diving flags. There are some other flags that are used for emergencies and these are covered in this course in Chapter 10 under the Raising the Alarm section.

Diving

You need to be aware of two diver down flags that indicate the vessel has scuba divers below. You are required to stay 300 feet (100 meters) away from such a vessel.

In the USA, the red flag with a white strip is used.

USA dive flag.

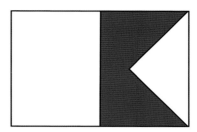

Dive flag—rest of the world.

In most of the rest of the world, the Code A flag is used.

Sound-Making Devices

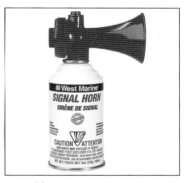

Sound-making devices are extensively used as warning devices and for maneuvering announcements on larger ships.

An important note is to always have a loud sound horn near and accessible within 2 to 3 seconds of the helmsperson. This simple self-imposed rule WILL prevent a collision at some point in your sailing life.

Sound horn.

Flares

Flares are used to communicate an emergency situation. There are many types of flares used for different situations: rocket, hand-held, smoke, water dye, and LED.

Electronic Communications

> ## A Thought
>
> Imagine if humans had 16 fingers instead of 10. We'd all be able to grasp hexadecimal code a lot easier. Just sayin!

Morse code uses a long blip and a short blip. Combinations of these blips represented a letter. A fast human Morse coder could send ten letters in a few seconds, but the accuracy depended also on the human receiver's ability to decode the message just as quickly.

Nowadays, gigabytes of data can be sent in a second as a digital signal. It is all a complete wow, and we've seen this invention of technology, including all the working satellites launched into orbit, during our lifetimes. Signals travel and are coded and decoded at the speed of light.

All these signals are for the benefit of us communicating with one another. AND the field of Electronic Communication continues to explode. Knowing the importance of knowledge and data, sailors have embraced technology. Even the laggards and Luddites carry an iPhone in their pocket to communicate with their grandchildren via video over 4g.

Although telecommunications technology is improving quickly, people at sea need to know many maritime-specific communications:

- Mariners need to be able to communicate with other ships of any size or nationality.
- Mariners need to be able to receive and send urgent maritime safety information.
- Mariners need to be able to send or receive distress alerts in an emergency to or from rescue coordination centers ashore and nearby ships anywhere in the world.

So given all the above, the following is a discussion of what you should expect operating a small keelboat close to shore.

VHF Radios

VHF (Very High Frequency) radios are a primary source of radio communications between vessels and shore installations. And VHF radios are, more important, a primary source of communication for announcing and coordinating operations during an emergency. Most maritime safety organizations monitor VHF radio signals and specifically channel 16, which is the international distress, safety, and calling channel.

If you put out a distress signal on channel 16, the chances of it being heard by someone who can rescue you is almost 100%. The "almost" lies in the distance VHF signals can travel and landmass obstructions in the way.

VHF is essentially a line-of-sight system, since radio waves don't bend very much to follow the curvature of the earth. Sometimes the signal can reflect and refract around landmasses to advantage, but mostly if there is a landmass in the way, you cannot expect your signal to get through. However, for most reliable communication, the VHF antenna must "see" the antenna of a distant station. Therefore, antenna height is more important in determining the range than radio wattage. The effective useful range, then, of a VHF radio is 20 to 25 miles for ship to shore and

10 to 15 miles for ship to ship. The distance a VHF signal can reach between ship and shore installations is usually a bit farther, since the ground-based antenna is higher.

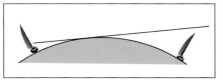

VHF signal.

Fixed-Mount VHF Radios

Fixed-mount units are just that—they are permanently fixed into your boat and are usually high wattage up to 25 watts. They gain their power from the house battery system.

Handheld VHF Radios

VHF handhelds also offer many of the same features found on fixed-mount units. They offer portability in the same way a cordless phone allows more mobility at home. A handheld radio may be just what you need for use in a dinghy, small boat without electrical systems, or as an emergency backup for your boat's radio. Handhelds have a maximum output of six watts. Due to their short antennas, they have a limited range of five miles.

VHF radio.

A significant increase in range can be achieved by connecting an external antenna or using a telescoping antenna mounted to the handheld radio. Battery life varies with the size of the battery pack. Many models have optional battery packs with

longer operating times, greater transmitting power, or both. Some have battery saver circuits that turn off the receiver to save power. The battery life of a handheld can be increased by switching from full transmit power to one watt of transmit power.

A battery-charging system should be made available on the vessel.

Check out a handheld VHF/DSC radio. Scan the code above for a product review from West Marine.

Channel 16

Channel 16 is the most important VHF channel for sailors. It is essential for all emergencies. The United States Coast Guard and most other countries' coast guard systems monitor channel 16, 24 hours a day, 7 days per week.

Channel 16 is designated as the single channel to be constantly operational by all vessels at sea. This channel is a sailor's best link for communicating problems with other vessels or ground-based stations.

Operating VHF radios is easy, but there are protocols to follow. One thing to keep in mind is that the sender and the receiver cannot talk at the same time. This is often difficult to remember in an emergency. Transmissions should be kept short and cover only vital issues.

You can find the proper procedure for using your VHF—Channel 16—radio in an emergency in Chapter 10.

General Calls to Other Ships or Shore

You can refer to the Wikipedia marine VHF Channels CG website for a table of VHF Channels for the UK, USA, Canada, Australia, New Zealand, and Finland.

Each channel has a specific use. Note carefully the channels you as a recreational noncommercial boater can use to communicate. Each Channel operates on a different VHF frequency. Here is a summary for the USA:

- **Channel 09** - Boater Calling. Commercial and Noncommercial.
- **Channel 16** -International Distress, Safety, and Calling. Any ships that are required to carry a VHF radio. Global Coast Guards, and most coast stations, maintain a listening watch on this channel.
- **Channel 68** - Noncommercial traffic
- **Channel 69** - Noncommercial traffic
- **Channel 71** - Noncommercial traffic
- **Channel 72** -Noncommercial (Intership only)
- **Channel 78A** - Noncommercial traffic
- Special Note: **Channel 70** is for Digital Selective Calling (DSC) only. No voice is allowed. See below for a DSC discussion.
- **WX1** through **WX7** are weather broadcasting channels. They are listen only. No transmission is possible. The frequency range is slightly higher than any of the Channels 1 through 88.

All others are for port operations, commercial traffic government, and the like. They should not be used by recreational boaters. Note in particular that Channel 70 is for DSC distress signals. No voice is allowed on channel 70. Sometimes you'll see an A and B switch. A is used in the USA and internationally. B is used only outside the USA. (B is sometimes labeled as "International.")

Procedure for Hailing a Ship by Radio

You may use channel 16 to hail a ship or shore station, but if you do so, you **must, must be brief!** We recommend this same procedure be used over channel 9, if channel 9 is used as a calling channel.

A hailing example:

Blue Duck: "*Mary Jane*, this is *Blue Duck*" *(the name of the vessel being called may be said 2 or 3 times if conditions warrant)*

   Mary Jane: "*Blue Duck*, this is *Mary Jane*. Reply 68" *(or some other proper working channel)*

   Blue Duck: "68" or "Roger"

   Both switch to channel 68 (as an example). Have the conversation. End each turn with "over." End conversation with your station name and "out."

Operator's License

Some countries in the Mediterranean require that you have a VHF operator's license before entering their waters. If chartering a yacht, the charter company is required to ensure you have the same before heading out.

DSC – Digital Selective Calling

Scan the code, at right right for a quick introductory video on DSC.

   Digital Selective Calling, or DSC, is particularly excellent for distress signals. When the red distress button is activated, it automatically broadcasts an encoded digital distress call that will be picked up by all nearby vessels equipped with DSC. The designated VHF channel for DSC transmissions is 70. Therefore, you cannot use channel 70 for any reason other than DSC calls. The radio then switches to channel 16 for following voice communication. Since DSC uses VHF, it also is limited in range. The advantage is that it can send digital data that can be received much clearer than a garbled voice. The data sent in an emergency situation will include a distress signal, the GPS location, the vessel information, and, much like pre-formatted texts, conditions like "sinking" can be included.

   If the radio is interfaced with GPS, it will also automatically broadcast the distressed vessel's position. All DSC radios have an input connector protocol that allows GPS data input. If you have a GPS and a DSC radio, CONNECT THEM.

Many DSC radios now include GPS as a feature. To use DSC, you must obtain a MMSI (Maritime Mobile Service Identity) number. You may do so free of charge at this web address: http://www.boatus.com/mmsi.

Note that DSC signals on VHF radios are still limited to VHF ranges. But through the network of DSC listening vessels in the area, your distress is likely to be heard. For this reason, if your vessel is fitted with DSC, you are required to have the device on when you are on board.

Scan the code at right for a video that talks more in depth about DSC radios.

Telephones

Ordinary cell phones often work well within their "cell" areas. Cell range is approximately line of sight and will vary with the cellular telephone provider.

However, Maritime Rescue centers do not recommend relying on cellular phones as a means of communication during an emergency. First, who are you going to call and do you have their phone number? You can't speak to the helicopter to coordinate the rescue via cell phone. The best you might manage is to call your mother-in-law (why she is on speed dial we don't know) and tell her to call the authorities. Then, you're expecting her to write down a latitude and longitude number?

Bottom line: make sure your vessel has an up-to-date VHF unit with DSC.

EPIRB

Pronounced "*e-purb*," an EPIRB is an acronym for Emergency Position Indicating Radio Beacon and is an emergency communication device that, when activated, continually emits signals to be picked up by satellites that then can direct rescue efforts. They float and are practically indestructible. Some now provide two-way communications.

As soon as an EPIRB is activated, usually by immersion in water, its signal is received by satellites and is rebroadcasted to ground stations or other ships equipped with receivers.

Some EPIRB models interface with Global Positioning Satellites (GPS) and thus pinpoint the location of the EPIRB. Today the EPIRB should definitely be considered an essential piece of electronic equipment for all offshore sailing.

EPIRB.

As with most electronic gear, the costs have dropped while their performance and reliability have improved. For sure, you are now no longer alone on the big oceans.

Personal Overboard Locator Beacon (POLB)

Personal overboard locator beacons are electronic tether devices worn by each crewmember, dog, cat, etc. When a POLB goes overboard, it starts transponding and sending alerts. The frequencies and alerts depend on the type of system. Some go via satellite, some via VHF/DSC.

AIS

The **Automatic Identification System (AIS)** is an automated tracking system used on ships and by Vessel Traffic Services (VTS) for identifying, locating, and tracking vessels. With an AIS unit on board, you can see if a ship is a threat to your current course and position. AIS information supplements marine radar, which continues to be the primary method of collision avoidance for water transport. Information provided by AIS equipment, such as identification, position, course, and speed (or at anchor), can be displayed on a screen for analysis by the watch person.

AIS operates at 161.975 MHz on the VHF band. Currently, only ships over 300 gross tonnage or passenger ships of any size are required to broadcast AIS information about their vessel. However, many recreational vessels now have opted to broadcast AIS for safety reasons; but many also don't. Thus, you're not going to get an accurate picture of all traffic with AIS. Therefore, AIS should not be considered an automatic collision avoidance system, but rather a collision risk determination with known AIS transponding targets. Keep in mind that if you're transmitting an AIS signal, then large ships have a better chance at seeing you, even if you are way out at sea, which creates some peace of mind.

In 2007, a new class B standard of AIS was introduced, which enabled a new generation of low-cost AIS transducers and thus triggered recreational mariners to invest in the AIS technology for their vessels. A third class is a receive-only AIS, meaning you can see information about them, they can't see you.

The transmitting AIS units (A and B) require a GPS transponder unit to collect your GPS position in order to transmit.

Scan the code at right for an excellent summary of the AIS technology.

Radar

Radar stands for **Ra**dio **D**irection **and R**anging. The acronym was coined by the U.S. Navy in 1940 during World War II.

While the electronics of Radar are pretty complicated, the principle is quite simple. When you send out a signal and measure the time (t) for an echo to come back, the distance (D) to the object reflecting the signal is found by:

D= c x t/2

where c = the speed of the signal.

In the case of radio waves: c = the speed of light = 299,792,458 m/sec.

It's pretty amazing that we have electronics that can measure time differences at those kinds of speeds. For example, if an object is 1 Nautical mile (1852 m) away, the time for the reflection to come back is:

t= 2 x D/c

= 2 x 1852 / 299,792,458

= 12 microseconds

= 12 millionths of 1 second

= wow!

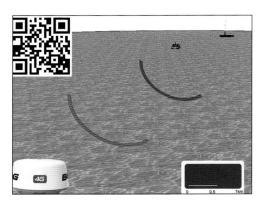

Radar.

But even better than that, the electronics can distinguish things that are 10 meters apart from the time differential. Double wow!

With Radar, you can "see" weather systems approaching, landmasses, and other vessels even if you cannot see them. Just a note however: the Rules for Prevention of Collision at Sea DO NOT allow for the replacement of a visual lookout with Radar (or AIS for that matter).

Global Positioning System (GPS)

Although the GPS is used as a navigation device, it is also a form of communication to the vessel. Thus we include it here. It's pretty interesting stuff.

> **Deep Thoughts**
>
> Imagine if in the 1700s, John Harrison gave Captain James Cook a few satellites and an iPad loaded with a Navionics App instead of a chronometer. Oh man! Cook would have probably taken about 20 minutes to master the concepts. Us? It'll take a little study.

Global Navigation Satellite Systems (GNSS)—Global Positioning Systems (GPS)—give navigators unique real-time tools, but there are a few things to learn before jumping in. Don't just assume that a GNSS will do the job for you once you're out there. Now's the place and time to understand the power of knowledge and the depth of information such a device can give to you.

GPS stands for global positioning system. It uses a network of satellites in orbit.

A GPS receiver calculates its position by precisely timing the signals sent by GPS satellites high above the Earth.

Today, it is probable that besides your main chart plotter, you will have multiple other GPS devices on your vessel, things like you and your crew's phone and tablet devices. So reliability and redundancy is high. Additionally, there are multiple satellites being used. The more satellites the device can see, the more confidence in the accuracy of the position. A GPS device will allow you to see how many satellites it is seeing and will thus give you its own confidence value. This value is called the Horizontal Dilution of Precision (HDOP).

It is also unlikely that multiple satellites go offline at the same time. So given all the above, it is reasonably safe to say that relying on GPS navigation is a sane(ish) thing to do. HOWEVER, given that you can't breathe water, it is NOT prudent for the following reasons:

- GPS units can go out
- Your batteries and thus recharging ability is down
- Your aerials fail
- You roll in a storm and everything is shorted out
- There is a solar flare interruption of the satellite signals
- You are struck by lightning and everything is fried (it happens)

In addition, the information stored in a GPS digital chart is only as good as the information originally entered. Older paper charts are scanned and digitized into a chart plotter. The accuracy of your information presented by the GPS will depend on the age of the charts.

Prudence means regularly maintaining a logbook of your positions, double-checking your position on a paper chart, and using visual aids of landmarks, buoys, depth soundings, and oil platforms. At sea, a prudent captain will contact passing container ships for a double check of position.

It is thus seen that knowledge of both paper charts and how to use them, combined with electronic chart information, is the wise thing to do.

GPS and the Speed of Light

In 1638, Galileo is often credited with being the first scientist to try to determine the speed of light. His method was quite simple. He and an assistant each had lamps that could be covered and uncovered at will. Galileo would uncover his lamp, and as soon as his assistant saw the light, he would uncover his. By measuring the elapsed time until Galileo saw his assistant's light and knowing how far apart the lamps were, Galileo reasoned he should be able to determine the speed of the light. His conclusion: "If not instantaneous, it is extraordinarily rapid." Galileo deduced that light travels at least ten times faster than sound.

(Source credit: http://www.speed-light.info/measure/speed_of_light_history.htm.)

The speed of light was further refined over the centuries. In 1862, Leon Foucault determined the speed of light was 299,796 km/s. Today the adopted speed of light is 299,792.458 km/s—only 4 km/s different from Foucault's.

Each satellite continuously transmits messages that include:

- the time the message was transmitted, and
- satellite position at time of message transmission.

The receiving unit uses the time differences between the messages from each satellite. From this, it determines the transit time of each message and thus computes the distance to each satellite using the speed of light. These distances are used to compute the location of the receiver using spherical geometry equations.

Basic GPS measurements yield only a position, and neither speed nor direction. However, most GPS units can automatically derive velocity and direction of movement from two or more position measurements over time.

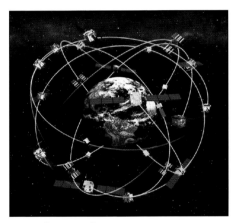

A satellite in orbit.

Notice from the above that the device on your vessel does not communicate back to the satellite. The information received from the satellite: time of day and satellite location is sufficient.

A final wonder in regard to this whole concept is that we have instruments that can measure difference in distance using light traveling this fast. It's incredible, and kudos go to all the engineers (and begrudgingly the politicians) who made all this possible and as a free service to the world.

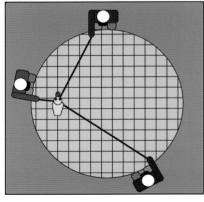

How a GPS works.

Simplified: How GPS Works

It's pretty simple, really. Place three people around the edge of a duck pond at known angles from one another. Each holds one end of a piece of string with the other end tied to a rubber duck. By knowing the length of each piece of string, you could very accurately determine the duck's exact and **unique** position inside that circle.

With GPS, the length of string is the time it takes for the signal to get from a satellite to you. By knowing the time traveled for at least three satellite signals, the software inside the device can accurately calculate your unique position on earth at the particular moment in time. One second later, the same calculation can be done and a new position established. Armed with this information, the device can report speed and direction findings. Note that there are no signals that go from the GPS device to the satellite. The GPS device receives a time-stamped signal from each satellite. Comparing the differential in time each signal reports to the GPS device gives the length of the string.

A Plane from the Australian Hydrograpic Office Gathers Depth Data

Hydrographic office airplane.

Electronic Charts

GPS charts use the same data accuracy concept as computers' GIGO, which stands for Garbage In/Garbage Out. Initially, when digital first came on the scene, digital maps were created from paper charts, and paper charts were created from the latest information available. Going back a few more years, charts had serpents and giant squid—these could equally have been digitized. This means your digital charts are only a representation of known information and not all information is exactly known. In some cases, chart information still exists based upon sextant celestial navigation information from way back, i.e., of course we know where The Kingdom of Tonga is, but are the positions of rocks and reefs known exactly within 6 ft?

Today, many coastal areas ARE accurately charted using high-tech hydrographic equipment. Airplanes beaming red and green lasers down into the waters can digitally document with ridiculous accuracy the landscape of the bottom. Red lasers bounce off the surface and green lasers bounce off the bottom. The time differential tells the depth. Using this method, a pass by an airplane at 250 knots can digitize a swath of coastline 250 meters wide. The data collected hundreds of terabytes detailing rocks the size of a basketball on the bottom. This data then reduced down to create a very accurate chart. The trouble is, we don't know if the digital chart we are using was created from a paper chart with serpents or from lasers.

Another example to keep in mind was an accident report of a yacht hitting a long pier at night. It wasn't on the digital chart. The reason was that the pier was built after the yachtsman had updated his digital charts. And think of a recent sunken vessel that is not on the charts. More than likely, however, both the pier and the sunken vessel will have been lighted with a navigational light / marker / buoy (an ATON, or Aid to Navigation).

The lessons brought forth here emphasize that sailing instruments do not replace a sailor's natural senses; they help enhance and validate them.

Ultimately, we must also be cognizant that electronically stored information is subject to failure via lightning strikes, coffee spills, a knock down, battery failure, hard drive failures, aerial failures, solar flares, satellite failures, etc. Essentially, a lot can go wrong with disastrous consequences if you're not thinking. So always make sure that you back up your positions on paper in your logbook and on the chart.

Interesting Question

A situation from a recent Bareboat Charter trip to St. Vincent and Bequia Island in the Caribbean. One of the following statements is true:

1. We got up enough speed to ram right over the top of an island.
2. There is a giant tunnel through this island.
3. The island doesn't exist but is shown on the digital charts.

Electronic navigation error.

The truth is that the island does not exist, and for purposes of this article and electronic navigation discussions on NauticEd, I purposely steered the boat right through it. There was no change in depth as we went through it. It is not named nor does it have a height listed on the chart, but all the other islands do list a height.

Chapter 8
Navigation

Introduction

For the most part, you use navigation skills when operating away from your home port. This chapter assumes you are learning and growing your skills somewhat close to home during daylight hours. Navigation represents a lot of mathematics and spatial understanding. It is a deep and seemingly endlessly complex topic, and more than you need when you are just getting started. . . .

Eventually, understanding these complexities is essential to being a responsible skipper. You should not rely on line of sight sailing. There are other sinister factors at play like, fog, currents, tides, storms, and electronic and mechanical breakdowns. Remember, you are in command of a vessel and responsible for the lives of others. Your crew rightly or wrongly assumes when they step on your boat that you know what to do in any situation that may present itself.

For this reason, we highly recommend that you take a good international Coastal Navigation course. It will get you out there and home safely. NauticEd offers such a course online.

However, even when getting started, it is important to recognize the various day marks you will see while on the water. These day marks guide you and keep you out of trouble; they are called Aids to Navigation (ATONs).

Aids to Navigation (ATONS)

ATONS is the acronym for Aids to Navigation. These aids include buoys, lights, light houses, and markers, among others.

Lateral Mark

A lateral buoy, also called a lateral post or lateral mark, is defined by the International Association of Lighthouse Authorities (IALA) as a sea mark used in maritime pilotage to indicate the edge of a channel.

Each mark indicates the edge of the safe water channel in terms of port (left-hand) or starboard (right-hand).

A vessel heading into a harbor and wishing to keep in the main channel should:

- keep port marks to its port (left) side, and
- keep starboard marks to its starboard (right) side.

And obviously a vessel heading out of a harbor should proceed opposite to the above.

For aid of memory, it is prudent to learn only what you should do when entering a harbor. Then you just apply the opposite when exiting. The last thing you want to do is to get flustered at night and try to remember which is which. Just learn one of the entering harbor mnemonics presented below.

Lateral Marks are not necessarily used solely in a harbor. They are also used in a river or coastal waterway. Logically for rivers, the upstream direction is treated the same as entering a harbor. For Coastal waterways, you need to check the chart to determine which way is considered "returning."

The International Association of Marine Aids to Navigation and Lighthouse Authorities (IALA) has established an international agreement on colors and shapes, using two systems, IALA-A and IALA-B, that depend on where you are. It is of course crucial you know which system is in effect where you are sailing.

The following is a guide to understanding the Aids to Navigation in the USA.

You absolutely must learn the difference between IALA-A and IALA-B and where they are used. Particularly if you are going chartering in various parts of the world. But don't worry, they are easy. All you have to do is remember the mnemonic **"Red, Right, Returning"** under the IALA-B system (North, Central, and South America; and Japan, Korea,

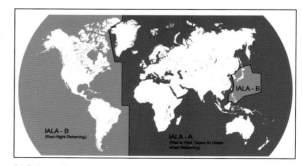

IALA regions.

and the Philippines). That's it! So, for example, under IALA-B, when you are returning from sea into the channel (or going upstream), keep the red markers on your right. In the case of the preferred channel, take notice of whatever color is on top. That is, if red is on top, keep the marker on your right for the preferred channel. Red Right Returning! Right?

If you live in under the IALA-A system, just remember Red to Red and Green to Green when returning. So when you are returning from sea into the channel (or going upstream), keep the green markers facing your green light and the red markers facing your red light. Our advice is to only learn one of these that suits you best. Then just apply the opposite logic/mnemonic when visiting a different IALA system.

A mnemonic to remember the shapes and colors for IALA-B that is commonly used is "even nuns blush red". Meaning nuns have even numbers and are red.

Safe Water Marks

A safe water mark is shown below, although it may not necessarily be this shape but is more characterized by white and red vertical marks. They are not numbered but may be lettered. The letters have no significance other than individual identification.

Special Purpose Marks

Special purpose marks are yellow and are used to mark such areas like anchorages, dredging and survey operations, and fishnet areas. They vary in shape from cans to balls to day boards.

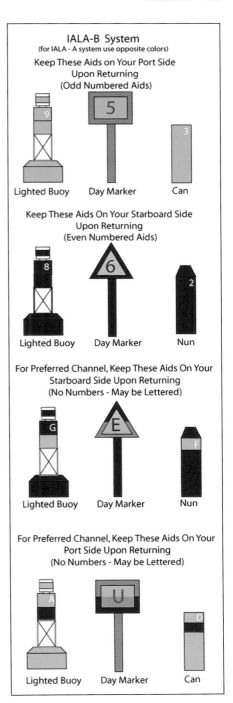

IALA-B System.

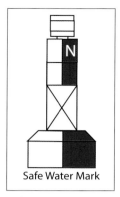

Safe Water Mark

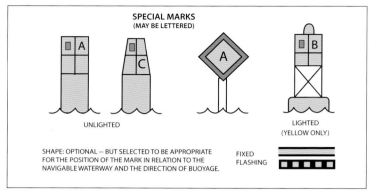

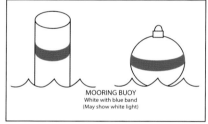

Safe Water.   Special Purpose.

Mooring Buoys

Mooring buoys for recreational boats are white with a blue stripe. If they are lighted, they exhibit a fixed white light. They may be a can shape or spherical.

MOORING BUOY
White with blue band
(May show white light)

Isolated Danger

Mooring ball.

Isolated danger marks bear a black strip on top of a red strip. They may be lettered for individual identification. The chart marks show "BR" (for black red) followed by the letter designation if it exists.

Putting It All Together

The diagram in the QR Code is a simple example of how you might navigate a channel in an IALA-B area.

And again—if you live in or plan to visit an IALA-A area, then just swap these colors. Don't stress too much—there used to be 30 different systems worldwide until the formation of IALA and international acceptance.

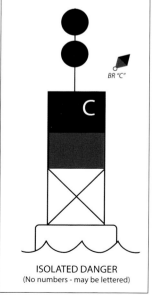

ISOLATED DANGER
(No numbers - may be lettered)

Isolated Danger.

Cardinal Marks

Various countries also use Cardinal marks. While not prevalent in the USA, you will see them in other places, including the Caribbean.

Cardinal marks tell you on which side there is safe passage around a hazard. For example, a North Cardinal mark will tell you to pass to the north of the mark for safe passage.

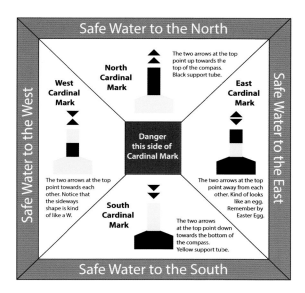

Cardinal Marks, and which side is safe.

Lights on ATONS

Lights are installed on **some** ATONS. These lights have different colors and different flash sequences that all mean different things. Some mean danger, some are safe water marks, while some guide you into the channel. We recommend that you become an expert at day sailing first before venturing out at night, whereby you will need to first study the meanings of these lights.

Electronic Navigation

Chances are that within 10 m (30 ft) of you right now there are 2 to 3 GPS-enabled life-saving devices. Those are your iPhones and iPads, Android phones and tablets, and perhaps even your watch. Given that these are so accessible, it would be irresponsible for even a rudimentary introductory boating course to not include the basics of using these devices to get you home or navigate out of a bad situation.

So the trick is now to get you to download a Navigation App and begin to use it on your device. It is not mandatory, but we think you'll have fun with it.

It seems like we all end up in the British Virgin Islands sometime, so you'll need your mobile device now for this section. We are going to work with the Navionics Caribbean and South America Electronic Chart.

iPhone	iPad (High Definition)
Android Phone	Android Tablet

Here are the iPhone, iPad, and Android links

The BVI

First let's get the lay of the land of the BVI. Click on an island to zoom in, then click on the home button to zoom out.

Next, here is an animation using the iPad. Start by tapping the Play button, then continue following the instructions or hit the CONT. button.

You will first measure the distance from the Road Town outer navigation markers to The Indians (one of the best places in the BVI to go snorkeling and often the first stop for charterers visiting the BVI).

Then you will Start the navigation, and you will see a data window pop up, which shows Speed, Track, and Distance. The Skipper will exit from Road Town, then turn onto the correct track to sail directly in a straight line to The Indians.

The great thing about the iPad is that it shows your track in a red line ahead of you. This is your real projected Course Over Ground (COG). It is not your heading because the iPad has no way of knowing which way your boat is pointing, but it does know based on previous GPS positions where it has been and so projects a track out in front. So for wherever you need to go, you just turn the boat until the iPad projected track lands on your destination, then keep following that course. This is your real direction of movement of the boat no matter what the current or leeway. Kinda feels like cheating, but it's not. Note, however, the currents and leeway change, and so you need to check often to make sure the red line is still landing over your destination. You also need to be very aware that your projected track is safe with no reefs, rocks, islands, or continents in the way. To do this, you should zoom all the way in and follow the track checking for hazards.

There is a lot more to know about electronic navigation. This is just enough for now to get you home.

Chapter 9
Anchoring and Mooring

Introduction

Ensuring that your boat is in the same place you left it is a very important skill. When anchoring, there are many factors to consider: depth under keel and surrounding area depth, tidal currents, low tide depth, other boats nearby, wind speed and direction changes, type of bottom, and length of stay. All factors play into your anchoring decisions.

Why Anchor?

There are many reasons for anchoring your boat:

Anchored in Corsica.

- Emergencies
- You are on an extended sailing trip
- You love warm romantic evenings under the stars
- Lunch in a gorgeous bay
- The kids want to go swimming (yourself included)
- Extreme hunger and your need to catch a snapper
- You have butter, garlic, and mango, and it would go really nice with a barbequed snapper
- Just because

Sometimes the "just becauses" in life are the best reasons.

While we might be able to forgo lunch in the bay, as a responsible skipper you have to understand that emergencies do arise (often), and thus anchoring knowledge beyond "dropping the hook" is absolutely essential.

Those types of emergencies include:

Safely anchored: a Beneteau First 20.

- Medical needs
- Gale force winds and waves that force you to hide it out behind shelter
- Engine failure (in current even worse)
- Fog
- Tired crew
- Rigging failure

Given the "whys" above, a "wise" sailor will carry at least two sets of anchors.

Types of Anchors

Anchor design has been the focus of much research over thousands of years, and as a result, there are now many different kinds to choose from. Selecting which anchor to use is often a matter of good sailor's judgment combined with experience.

Weight is a big factor in selecting an anchor. The weight of the anchor must match your boat's size. Most ships stores will help you do this matching.

Below are a few common types and comments about them.

-  Danforth: A pre-W.W. II lightweight anchor used extensively by various landing craft. It has a very high holding power compared to its weight. Some are made from aluminum. It is easy to deploy and store. Holds best in sand, mud, and clay. Poor in grassy bottoms.

-  CQR: An example of "plow" anchors. Invented in the 1930s we can only recommend this anchor as lawn art.

-  Bruce: A British design that rights itself when it hits the bottom. Intended to reset itself should it be pulled loose. Relatively easy to break loose from its setting. Useful in sand, rocks, and mud.

-  Plough-type anchors: Seemingly the best all-around anchor type. They dig in and hold well. They may not be the best in really, really soft mud, but great for regular mud, sand, and gravel.

-  Fisherman or kedge: Invented over 1,000 years ago, probably. Reminds us of the classics 1800s movies like "Master and Commander." It is mostly seen in gardens outside seafood restaurants.

Scan the top QR code for some photos of anchors mounted on sailboats in a marina.

As you peruse boating magazines and walk through marine stores, you will see an array of anchors, each with its promotional material. This information will help you decide on the type(s) of anchors you wish to carry.

Scan the code to the right for a short clip we took at the Annapolis Boat Show of some anchors in a tub.

Rode and Scope

Rode

To hold a sailboat in one place relative to the bottom, the anchor must naturally be attached to the vessel. This is accomplished by using "rode," which is either all chain or a combination of rope or line and chain. Rode, then, is the stuff in the middle between the anchor itself and the boat. In this discussion, the words rope and line are commonly interchanged. Some people say "anchor rope" and "anchor line" when they mean the rope part of the rode. Then there are the people who say there are no ropes on a boat. But from the rigging discussion earlier, we know that is not true.

The "bitter end" is the opposite end of the rode from the anchor.

Scope

The word "scope" is the ratio of the length of the rode compared to the depth of the water the anchor is set in.

Scope must be understood. Like gravity, scope is a universal law. You cannot simply dangle your anchor on the bottom. For all chain, the length you let out should be at least 4 times the depth of the water. Take into account when looking at the depth on your depth meter that you have an offset from the keel. For example, if the depth reads 15 feet on the meter, the real depth will be 20 feet if your offset is set to 5 feet.

Scope, then, is the amount of rode you let out divided by the depth. For example, in 20 feet of water your scope will be 4 if you let out 80 feet of chain.

Just as an aside, you get a weird sense of lengths when anchoring. Consider this: if your boat is 25 feet long, 50 feet is only 2 boat lengths, 100 feet is 4 boat lengths. To gain experience and confidence with this concept, consider snorkeling the anchor after you have laid it.

If your rode is made up of chain and rope, you should use at least 6 times the depth of the water. In higher wind conditions, you might elect for a 7:1 (7 times the length of rode than the depth of water) or even a higher ratio; or in lighter winds, you might think a 5:1 ratio is appropriate.

In general, **more scope is better** when it comes to holding power. But you will always have some balancing decisions to make around scope. Some factors to consider in your decision include:

- the harbor is crowded
- some boats may be using all chain (which will have less swing)
- your own swing
- predicted night wind shifts and strengths
- tidal change
- the amount of chain before rope on your rode
- the closeness to shore or underwater rocks

Because of all these factors, it is best that you set a GPS anchor alarm and a depth change alarm to warn you if you have moved and multiple time alarms just to get up multiple times in the night to check.

Why use a large scope? Because an anchor relies on the flukes being dug horizontally in the bottom, not hooked under a rock. Thus, the rode must continuously lie across the bottom while pulling on the anchor. The heavy chain acts to keep the rode on the bottom. The more rode you let out, the greater the chance the rode stays lying

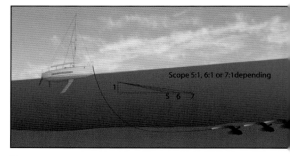

Proper scope.

Scope 5:1, 6:1 or 7:1 depending

horizontal in wind gusts. Wind gusts pull your boat backwards and inherently try to lift the rode up off the bottom. If you have sufficient length and weight of rode, the rode next to the anchor will remain lying horizontally across the bottom.

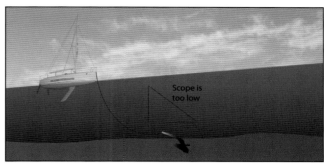

Scope too low.

The diagram to the right is an example of too little rode being let out. You can fairly much guarantee that your boat will "drag its anchor" at this scope.

Play the animation on the diagram below to see how a proper amount of rode keeps the rode laying horizontal in a wind gust.

The decision on rode configuration depends upon the anchor selected, sea bottom, water depth, the size of the vessel, weather conditions, and "gut level feelings." This gut feeling is important as a factor because there are so many unknown variables.

Letting out more rode gives better holding power, but this must be balanced with your diameter of swing should the wind change direction. This is why most sailors elect for tried-and-true ratios that work: 4 to 1 for all chain and 6 to 1 for chain/rope combination. But a watchful eye must be kept to ensure the anchor is not slipping across the bottom.

The path (curve) of the anchor rode from the bow to the anchor is mathematically a "catenary." The catenary is created by gravity pulling down on the rode. Since chain is much heavier than rope/line, the catenary shape is much different for chain

Anchoring animation.

than rope/line, as you might imagine. Chain tends to sit on the bottom for as much of its length as possible and because of this:

- The anchor is held flat, which gives it better holding ability.
- The curve is much greater, and therefore when the boat is hit by a wave the shock is taken up by the rising of the chain and not stretch in the rope/line.
- Abrasion on sharp rocks on the bottom is not an issue.
- It is heavy and also difficult to pull up without some sort of mechanical advantage such as a windlass.

Nylon line is good because of its elasticity and light weight. Chain is good because of its strength, weight, and ability to withstand abrasion.

Many vessels will have a combination of chain attached to the anchor and then nylon line that attaches to the vessel. The decision boils down to where you intend to anchor, and location, location, location.

A typical combination chain and line anchor rode is made up of one boat length of chain and 250 to 300 feet (80m to 100m) of nylon line. What then is the maximum practical depth to anchor in if a 6:1 scope ratio is desired? The depth is 300/6 = 50 feet (16m). That's not very deep!

Finally, you need a way to determine how much anchor line has been "paid out." A good suggestion is to mark the chain and/or nylon line at every 25 feet (7m). Ship stores carry a variety of markers for this purpose. Paint of different colors on the chain is good, and also many people use nylon tie wraps: 1 at 25 ft, 2 at 50 ft, and 3 tie wraps at 75 feet.

Here's a fun video where we dive down to the anchor and check its set; and a few other things we found on the bottom.

Anchor & Rode Inspection

Since your boat and life depend on your anchor's ability to hold your boat off the rocks, it's a good idea to ensure that the rode will not let you down.

At *least* every 6 months:

- Inspect the rode length for rust and abrasion
- Inspect the connections from rope to chain and chain to anchor
- Ensure that the pin in the D-ring connecting the chain to the anchor is secured tightly with stainless steel wire so it cannot work free
- Inspect the cleat that holds the rode to the boat to ensure it is solidly mounted
- Ensure that the end of the anchor line, called the "bitter end," is firmly attached to the vessel, usually to a special cleat located in or near the anchor locker
- Inspect the mounting of the windlass (if fitted)

Anchoring

Anchoring is not simply throwing a "hook" and letting out line. Although, after watching some sailors, this seems to be their theory. The best way to approach anchoring is to dissect it into a series of individual steps.

Anchoring is not always easy, even when you understand these "baby steps." Remember, anchoring is something you will always do without knowing all the factors. So do not be discouraged if your anchor does not hold each time.

Selecting a spot for the night or a shorter or longer stay is pretty important, and there are quite a few considerations.

Consider these

The biggest failures to safely anchor and properly hold an anchor are lack of attention to wind and tides, and poor "setting" of the anchor in the first place.

- Shelter from wind, swell, and waves
- Out of the way of traffic
- Sufficient depth of water around the entire 360-degree swing of the vessel if wind direction changes
- Rising and falling tide
- Changing current caused by tides
- Bottom conditions (good or poor holding ability compared to type of anchor)
- Prohibited anchoring area
- Cables and lines across the bottom. These almost always exist in a marina. But also check the charts for subsurface electric and telephone lines to an island or peninsula.
- Scope
- Make-up of your anchor line "rode." (All chain or chain/rope(line) combination?)

Wind

Expect the wind direction to change and expect the wind velocity to change.

Tide

The tide goes up and the tide goes down. A rising tide will reduce your scope and will reduce the ability for the rode to lie horizontally across the bottom. Scan the code at right for an animation.

An ebbing tide will increase your swing, putting you closer to shore, or land you on the bottom or rocks, or all three.

Setting

Use the proper amount of scope.

In general, do not try to anchor under sail, unless you are a very experienced sailor and conditions are ideal.

Motor into the area you wish to anchor in and select a potential spot. Now survey the possible dangers throughout the potential spot's swing area. Post a lookout at the bow to warn of any obstacles. This person may also be the one to lower the anchor or give instructions to the helmsperson.

Review the chart first, and keep an eye on the depth of water. Whenever anchoring near a shore, this depth can decrease in a hurry, risking running aground. Knowing the depth will also assist in determining rode.

Remember to be courteous to other vessels anchored before you. They do have "right of stay." This includes respecting distances, and keeping noise and commotion to a minimum. They will be watching you, often giving advice and encouragement. The pressure will be on.

Once at the "spot," ensure your boat is pointed into wind. Lower the rode slowly so that it does not "pile up" on the bottom at the same time the boat is reversing away downwind. Take care not to get your legs caught in the paying out rode. Proper communication between the person deploying the anchor and the helmsperson is essential. Once the proper amount is paid out, continue with slowly backing the boat. This will give the anchor a chance to "set" into the bottom. If you are lucky, it will set the first time; otherwise, several attempts may be needed.

Anchoring Example

For this example, consider anchoring in 12 feet of water below your keel with a chain/rope combination rode.

Using 12 feet of clearance, a 4 foot keel depth, a 4 foot bow to water height, and a 6:1 scope, you determine you need 120 feet of rode. (To anchor

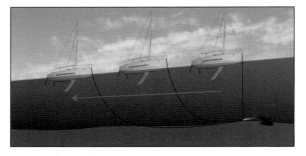

Setting the anchor.

in other depths, you will need to make appropriate accommodations and adjustments.)

Step One: Once you decide on a spot, circle around the area (with a 120 foot radius) so you are sure a 360 degree swing in the night will not ground you (consider tide changes).

Step Two: As you approach the selected anchorage, put the bow of the boat into the wind and prepare to drop the anchor at the predetermined spot.

Step Three: When the desired spot is reached, stop the boat and pay out the anchor rode until the anchor hits the bottom. It is important not to pile the chain all on top of itself.

Step Four: Begin backing the boat slowly and pay out the rode as required, maintaining a little back tension on the rode. When 120 feet of rode is reached, cleat off the rode.

Step Five: Setting the anchor happens when it digs into the sea bottom. When the anchor is set, the boat will stop moving back. You can also apply a little more reverse throttle to give the anchor a "good set." But don't overdo it.

Again, remember the ratios for the rode:

- All chain: use 4 to 1 ratio (or more)
- Line and chain: use 6 to 1 ratio (or more)

Notes:

- If you are staying on the boat, awake and aware, and anchoring for a short time, and the wind is light, you might consider lessening your scope
- Be aware that depending on the water depth, a 6:1 ratio can create a large diameter circle for your boat to swing around, which is sometimes not desirable
- In general, try to anchor shallower keeping in mind tide and swing

Swing

Your boat position is always downwind from the anchor. When the wind changes direction, your boat position changes. This change in position is called swing.

Swing should always be considered when anchoring, especially if anchoring overnight or leaving the boat alone. A change in wind can put your boat into a precarious situation by being too close to the shore or a rock or reef that was previously clear. As long as you don't anchor too close to other anchored boats, there is usually not a problem because those boats will also swing with the wind change.

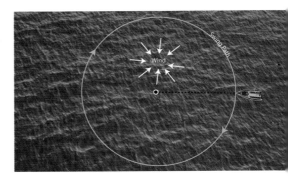

Swing.

Many times you'll find an area with mooring balls. Moorings are tied straight down to the sea floor, and thus boats tied to moorings swing less than anchored boats. Therefore, it is generally a very bad idea to anchor in a mooring field. The golden rule is always "consider your swing."

Consideration must be given to the tide. As the tide "ebbs" out, you not only get closer to the bottom, but your swing circle grows and the shore becomes closer. The diagram

Swing, another look.

above, top shows a boat's swing path with deep water and correct scope.

The diagram above, bottom shows that as the tide ebbed out, the scope increased as well as the swing path, bringing the boat dangerously close to the bottom and/ or shore.

Monitoring

After the anchor has set and adequate rode has been paid out, take time to ensure you are not drifting. And considering changing winds and tide height and tidal current, it is important to periodically monitor how well your anchor is set.

Check your anchor set manually and electronically. Do

Swing, another view.

this manually by sighting bearings to objects on shore and determining that they are constant. Note that the boat will swing back and forth with the wind, making it a little difficult to check that you are remaining steadfastly connected to the bottom. But, over time, you will get a feeling that through each successive swing, bearings to objects on the shore are not changing.

Using an electronic means will give you a more accurate determination of anchor set. If you have a GPS device, turn it on and turn on "show track." Observe over time the history track of your boat. If the tracks overlay one another, then you are holding steadfast. You can also use an anchor alarm on your depth meter. To do this, you set the maximum and minimum allowable depths. If the depth goes out of this range, the alarm sounds. There are also Apps for your mobile device. Here are a few:

DragQueen for iOS		Anchor Watch for iOS	
Drag Queen for Android		Anchor Watch for Android	

Lighting

The International Rules of Prevention of Collision at Sea govern the lighting requirements for anchoring. These are described in Chapter 5. Not only must you know your own lighting requirements, but you must know others' requirements in order to be able to identify them. We recommend that you revisit the rules often. Visit our Sailing Apps page to download the free NauticEd App. You can then review all the NauticEd Courses offline while you sit in the doctor's office or are stuck on an airplane.

For a sailboat at anchor, the requirement is one all-around (visible from 360 degrees) white light at the top of the mast. You may NOT leave on your green and red side lights or your white stern lights "for extra visibility." Those are running lights and indicate that you are NOT at anchor. A good idea, however, is to leave on a cabin light; but consider your batteries.

A further life-saving idea is to always have a powerful flashlight available within quick reach in the dark.

Multiple Anchors

There are occasions when more than one anchor will add safety and comfort. One possibility is to use one or two anchors from the bow, one from the stern, or both. The conditions requiring this will usually relate to anchoring in heavy weather, tight quarters, or not wanting your vessel to swing onto the beach. The photo to the right was taken in Corsica, where a tight cove made it necessary to anchor off the front and then secure two lines off the stern to large rocks on shore.

Multiple anchors.

Normally, the bow anchor is set first; then the stern anchor is placed using a dinghy to take it out to the desired spot. Then the crew on the vessel will pull the rode until the anchor sets. When doing this, you will want to ensure the anchor is indeed set.

In heavy weather, using two anchors off the bow may be prudent and desirable. The two rodes would make an angle of 45 to 90 degrees to the vessel's bow. Extreme care and thought are needed when using two anchors off the front. If the boat swings in the night, the anchor rodes will get tangled. A solution is a swivel ring.

In the diagram below, left, two anchors are set at 45 degrees. Notice the swing circle in this diagram compared to the diagram below, right, whereby the anchors are set at 90 degrees apart. 45 degree set anchors are best in heavy wind conditions, as each anchor takes half the load so long as the wind direction is constant.

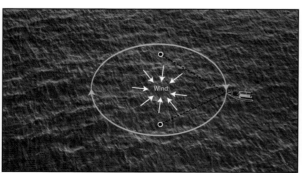

Swing with multiple anchors.

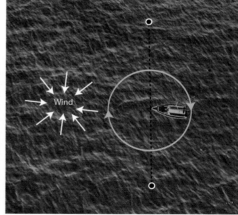

Bahamian anchoring.

90 degree set anchors are best used in light winds in tight quarters where swing room is a concern. This style of anchoring is called the Bahamian anchoring technique.

In every case, if possible, you should dive down to your anchor with a mask and snorkel to ensure it is set properly. You'll sleep a lot better in the night. Maybe not this time, but one time you will save your boat and possibly your life.

Innovative anchoring.

Anchoring Courtesy

After having safely and securely anchored your vessel, there are certain factors to contend with; most are common sense.

- Be courteous to those anchored around you; be quiet and mindful
- If you run your engine, be aware of potential carbon monoxide fumes
- Don't dump anything overboard in an anchoring/mooring field. Even a floating banana peel is unsightly for others
- Anchor using the same method as the other boats around you so your swing will match theirs with changes in direction of wind
- Don't anchor in a mooring field; the swing on a mooring line is much less than that of an anchor rode

Busy harbor: Hvar, Croatia.

Weighing Anchor

With an Engine

"Weighing the anchor" simply means raising it.

If raising the anchor is to be done by "hand," make certain the assigned crew members (who pull in the rode and raise the anchor) are physically able. This can be a physically demanding chore.

When the time comes to leave an anchorage, there are recommended procedures:

Step One: Ensure all gear is properly stored. Crew and passengers need to be alerted about procedures that will be taken. Ensure you have an agreed-upon set of hand signals between the crew member who is retrieving the anchor and the helmsperson.

Step Two: Start the engine and slowly motor toward the anchor, all the while pulling in the rode and placing it in the anchor locker. Do not let the rode drift under the vessel, as it could become entangled in the propeller, creating some real problems.

Step Three, Plan A: As the vessel moves over the spot where the anchor is—pull it up, if you can. Stop the vessel's forward motion as you continue pulling in the anchor. If you use an electric windlass to raise the anchor, be vigilant to ensure it is running freely.

Plan B: If the anchor is set hard and you cannot pull it in, you may need to use the vessel's forward motion to break the anchor loose. This means maintaining slight forward motion and cleating the rode as you pass over the spot. The theory is that the vessel's momentum will break loose the anchor. Be very wary of the strength of the cleat on your boat.

Plan C: If the anchor fails to break loose, due to rock formation, you can try to pull it out backwards by motoring to windward. The flatter the angle you pull the anchor out, the greater the chance of retrieval, so let out lots of rode when motoring to windward. Be conscious of the rode and propeller at all times.

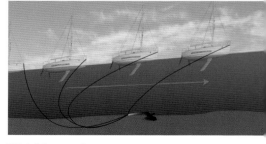

Weighing anchor.

Plan D: Try pulling the anchor out sideways. Let out lots of rode and motor across the wind on either side alternately.

Plan E: Persistence and various combinations of the above will normally work in your favor.

Tip: If you don't have a windlass and you're feeling a little tired, you can run the rode back to one of the winches atop the cabin.

Watch out that you're not stuck on a boat dock cable from a marina. In lakes, you might often be stuck on an old tree stump.

A variety of other techniques can be used when anchoring in rocky bottoms. One is attaching a line and a float to the backside of the anchor, making it possible to pull the anchor out backwards. However, this requires preplanning. If you're unsure of the bottom, then this might be a safety precaution.

The Anchor Rescue Device is an ingenious device that can save the day. You have to prepare for it, however, by purchasing the device and attaching to your anchor. Watch the video to the right.

If you decide to leave the anchor and rode for later recovery with a professional, don't cut the rode. Instead, let all the rode out and tie a floating bottle to the bitter end. This helps underscore the need to carry an extra anchor and rode for just such an unfortunate occasion.

The very worst scenario is that you will have to cut the rode and just get another one. However, keep in mind that anchors with rode are not cheap; they range from $US300 and up.

The best advice when weighing anchor is to remain calm and thoroughly think through your procedures before using them.

Without an Engine

At times, you may desire or need to retrieve the anchor without use of the engine. In this case, use the forward moving momentum of the boat rather than fighting the tension in the anchor rode. Pull the rode enough to get the boat moving forward; once the boat is moving, it will tend to continue moving forward and the rode will slacken, allowing you to pull in some more. Simple patience will save a lot of grunting and groaning.

Mooring

Mooring a vessel means attaching it to a float that is firmly anchored to the sea bottom. The key here is "firmly." Be cautious, as always. Mooring balls are subject to weather, corrosion, currents, and rotting lines that erode the mooring integrity. Thus, you should be aware of potentially being released during the night and dangerously drifting away. Always check your position during the night.

Some cities and communities provide great spots for short-term mooring. Some are free, some charge by the day. Many times, private individuals own a mooring. Thus, despite the mooring appearing to be available with no boat attached, you cannot tie up to it. Usually a private mooring ball will be marked, which you must respect. To obtain a mooring ball, check the local guide to see the procedure. Sometimes you can call the harbormaster and make a reservation beforehand. It is no fun to arrive at a spot where you intended to moor and discover there aren't any balls available. Other times in popular chartering areas, you just need to arrive early to be assured of a ball.

Scan the QR Code to the right to cycle through the various mooring buoys you will encounter.

Mooring Procedures

The procedure for tying to a mooring is theoretically very easy. You simply motor up and, using a boat hook—grab the float and attach to it. However, a minor problem can occur if you miss grabbing the float and have to do it again.

Mooring at sunset.

Moorings in popular harbors are often quite close together. If you have too much speed, you may have a potential collision problem; if you have too little speed and have to make a second attempt, make sure to maintain steerage.

Paramount is having established communication signals between the crewmember and the helmsperson. Grabbing a mooring ball needs to be planned. It is best achieved if you motor the vessel into the wind toward the mooring ball. The person grabbing the mooring line has a hook and must be strong enough to pull, or hold, the vessel should it be required.

The helmsperson needs to control speed and heading carefully. Once the mooring line is snagged, stop the vessel as quickly as possible, bring the mooring line on deck to secure.

Most often the actual mooring line that you bring onboard is a floating line attached to the mooring just below the ball. You simply hook the floating line and bring it aboard. When securing to a cleat, make sure it is a thick mooring line, not a thin messenger line.

Other times, you will encounter a steel ring in the top of the ball that you loop your own dock-line through. The problem with this configuration is that you cannot lift the ball out of the water with the boat hook, nor can you reach down to it from your forward deck. There is another method to get to the mooring ball if it is configured this way. Simply back up the boat to the mooring ball with your aft facing the wind. The linesperson has a better chance of reaching the mooring ball in this manner because the aft of the boat is not as high as the bow and the helmsperson and the linesperson can work together easier. It is preferable to use a long line that is already attached at one end to a forward cleat and run around the outside of everything (stays, lifelines, and bimini). The linesperson then simply walks the free end back to the forward deck, pulling in the slack, and attaches to the opposite cleat.

See our blog article on this by scanning the code above.

Safety Note: It is easier to go around and do it again than have your crew hurt themselves trying to hold the boat to the ball with the boat hook if the boat is drifting away. Train your crew to unhook the boat hook and let the ball go if it becomes difficult to hold.

Summary

Anchoring is an essential skill needed by all sailors. In some emergencies, it is the only option. It is also a desired skill that allows you to simply enjoy and share moments at sea. Getting proficient in anchoring takes knowledge and some practice, but the results are safety-enhancing and confidence-building.

- Use plenty of scope
- Check your swing
- Select the appropriate anchor
- Dive your anchor once it is set
- Check your depth regarding tide changes
- Ensure your scope will handle the tide change
- Watch proximity to others who may not swing as much as you

Flotilla at anchor.

- Watch the anchor set for several minutes to ensure it is not dragging
- Get up several times in the night to check your anchor
- Assume the wind direction will change

Chapter 10

Safety and Emergencies

Introduction

Emergency issues at sea extend from simple and almost funny episodes to major challenges that are extremely serious. When sailing goes well, life is good and we wish it would continue that way indefinitely. However, things can go wrong, and when they do sailors must be prepared—including calling for help.

The best strategy is to try to prevent emergencies from happening. This translates into the following:

- Practice safety. Safe behavior is an insurance against an emergency
- Learn the established rules. This is also a legal issue
- Know your vessel and its capabilities thoroughly
- Know your boat's equipment and maintain it
- Know yourself and your crew. This requires honesty, tact, and finesse.
- Prepare for possible problems. Have backup plans
- Learn how to read weather forecasts. Get a forecast every time you go out
- Use common sense aka good seamanship—(you know what that is)
- Be patient and courteous and always prudent

Safe practices and emergencies have much in common. Violate safety practices, and the probability of emergencies increases dramatically. Rules for proper use of vessels and behaviors have been established and agreed upon; when followed, emergencies are less likely to happen.

Safety Briefings

Many emergencies can be avoided through proper seamanship and knowledge. It is very important for the skipper to conduct a safety briefing before leaving the dock.

Scan the code to the right for a PDF checklist for you to print out and leave on your vessel for a checklist briefing.

Raising the Alarm

VHF

Procedure for VHF Channel 16 MAYDAY:

1. Switch to Channel 16. All Distress signals via VHF are initiated on Channel 16. This is a worldwide protocol.
2. Distress signal "MAYDAY," spoken three times.
3. The words "THIS IS," spoken once.
4. Name of vessel in distress (spoken three times) and call sign or boat registration number, spoken once.
5. Repeat "MAYDAY" and name of the vessel, spoken once with call sign.
6. Give the position of the vessel by latitude or longitude or by bearing (true or magnetic, state which) and distance to a well-known landmark such as a navigational aid or small island, or in any terms that will assist a responding station in locating the vessel in distress. Include any information on vessel movement such as course, speed, and destination.
7. Nature of distress (sinking, fire, etc.).
8. Kind of assistance desired.
9. Number of persons onboard.
10. Any other information that might help with the rescue, such as length or tonnage of the vessel, number of persons needing medical attention, color hull, cabin, masks, etc.
11. The word "OVER."

Stay by the radio if possible. You'll probably need to repeat information and answer further questions, particularly concerning your location.

For example:

MAYDAY-MAYDAY-MAYDAY
THIS IS BLUE DUCK - BLUE DUCK - BLUE DUCK

Call sign WA1234 MMSI number 233006734

MAYDAY BLUE DUCK

Call sign WA1234 MMSI number 233006734

OUR POSITION IS CAPE HENRY LIGHT BEARS 185 DEGREES MAGNETIC-DISTANCE 2 MILES

OUR CONDITION, WE HAVE STRUCK A SUBMERGED OBJECT

WE REQUIRE PUMPS, MEDICAL ASSISTANCE, AND TOW

THERE ARE THREE ADULTS AND TWO CHILDREN ONBOARD

ONE PERSON HAS A COMPOUND FRACTURE OF ARM

ESTIMATE CAN REMAIN AFLOAT TWO HOURS

BLUE DUCK IS THIRTY-TWO FOOT CABIN CRUISER - WHITE HULL - BLUE DECK HOUSE

OVER

Repeat at intervals until an answer is received.

Keep in mind that you may know how to make a MAYDAY call but your crew may not. At right is a code for a card you can download. Laminate it and zip tie to your VHF mic cord.

Calls Other than Distress on VHF

Urgency: "PAN, PAN, PAN" (*PAHN PAHN PAHN*). This is the International Urgency Signal and is used when a vessel or person is in some jeopardy of a degree less than would be indicated by Mayday.

Safety: "SECURITY, SECURITY, SECURITY" (*SAY-CURE-IT-TAY*). This is the International Safety Signal and is a message about some aspect of navigational safety or a weather warning. You will most often hear this from the Coast Guard. Listen and take appropriate actions if necessary. For example, perhaps a navigational aid has drifted off station or a tornado watch has been issued.

The United States Coast Guard's website and recommendations on VHF distress signals are available by scanning the code to the right.

Digital Select Calling (DSC)

Digital Select Calling is a means by which a digital distress signal is broadcasted via VHF Channel 70. Local Coast Guards monitor this in real time. It will report your GPS position, your vessel name and type, and the nature of your distress via a selectable text menu. However, there is a caveat; when you buy your DSC, you must register it and hook it up to your GPS unit. Instructions for this will be with the unit manual.

It is important to send a DSC signal first when in an emergency situation, because pertinent information such as your vessel type, name, and position is broadcasted digitally to all vessels in your VHF range vicinity, which gains more accurate and faster response times. After the DSC alert, you should send a voice alert. The Coast Guard monitors DSC 24/7. When they receive a DSC call, they are instantly given extremely accurate and helpful information to speed and enhance the success of the rescue.

The DSC will likely have a selection of prescribed alerts from which you can select. If time is short, holding the red distress button will send a standard distress signal with your location. To initiate the DSC, open the distress cover and either (1) hold the distress red button for 5 seconds for the standard message or (2) press the red distress button and then select the best suited message from the menu.

Watch this video interview with the Coast Guard.

Now watch how to send a distress signal.

The United States Coast Guard's website and recommendations on DSC distress signals is to the right.

EPIRB (Emergency Position Indicating Radio Beacon)

An EPIRB is an emergency device that will report a distress and your position to monitoring stations via satellite. It is automatically set off when immersed in water and has an automatic release mechanism from its mount if the boat is sinking. While not required in most countries, it is a must for every vessel. This video at right from the USA-based chandlery, West Marine, describes the EPIRB best.

Safety Equipment

There is a plethora of equipment specially designed for a variety of emergencies at sea. Some are inexpensive, while others are very costly. Determine your specific requirements by the kind of sailing you will be doing and the location. But don't be cheap. If you can't afford to buy safety equipment for your boat, you can't afford to go sailing. Any arguments?

Here is a PDF list of items you should keep onboard. Print it out and keep with your boat documents onboard. At least twice per season, go through the list and write the date you last checked the items for completeness.

Radar Reflectors

Large shipping traffic relies heavily on radar to avoid collision. Thus, given that you are small in comparison and don't want to be squashed like a bug, it is a good idea to do what you can to be seen. Radar reflectors are small, highly sensitive devices that you attach high up on your shroud lines (side stays). They are usually a small tube with metal pieces packed inside arranged at many different angles. They vastly increase the radar signal visibility of your vessel. These are especially important if your vessel is made of wood or GRP fiberglass, which tends to absorb rather than reflect radar signals.

Personal Flotation Devices

USA terminology uses PFD for Personal Flotation Devices, whereas much of the rest of the world uses Life Jacket. On this page, the terminology is used interchangeably.

You might think this topic is pretty boring and that all we're going to say is wear one. Actually, this is a pretty interesting topic and one that has progressed by the maritime safety organizations in a possibly unexpected direction. What was discovered was the biggest reason that people were not wearing a PFD is that they were uncomfortable. As soon as comfortable PFDs were designed and approved, drownings went down significantly—double significantly.

Thus, what we are not going to say is just "wear one." Rather, what we are going to say is "invest in a comfortable PFD and wear it." The biggest disservice that we do to children is to not have comfortable PFDs for them to wear. And you can imagine parents becoming so desperate for their child to enjoy boating that when the child starts whining because they are uncomfortable with an ill-fitting type 1 PFD, the parents take it off, thinking, "all is ok—we'll just pay extra attention." And that is the death of little Johnny. Please invest in your children's comfort and think of your purchase of a comfortable PFD as an investment in them enjoying boating—so you can go more.

Even if you don't have children, keep multiple, comfortable-fitting child size PFDs onboard. If children are coming out with you, ask the parents to ensure they have a properly sized comfortable PFD, one that the child can wear the entire time whilst onboard.

Buoyancy Ratings

The new rating system that PFDs/Life Jackets use is a Buoyancy Rating. It lists the amount of buoyancy force that a PFD can hold. Since we weigh less in water, it makes no sense to give a weight rating. On Earth, one Newton force is about 1/10 of a kilogram.

Life Jackets are rated in the following Buoyancy Rating Categories:
275 N - 150 N - 100 N - 50 N.

For example, a 150 N life Jacket provides 150 N for floating force. If a rock on the bottom of the ocean weighed 14 kg on a sunken weight measurement scale, then a 150 N rated life jacket would hold it afloat—barely. If the rock was 15 kgs (on a sunken weight measurement scale), then with a 150 N life jacket, it would have neutral buoyancy.

The average male weighing about 91 kg (200 lbs) requires about 4 kg (10 lbs) of buoyancy. The math here is performed using the person's body makeup of 80% water (neutral buoyancy) and 15% fat (positive buoyancy). 4 kg converts to 40 Newtons. Thus, the 150 Newtons is plenty for the average person and considered the minimum for an adult in off-shore conditions.

Regulations and Recommendations

- International (and all local) Regulations require that there be at least one PFD for every person on board. They all must be:
  - a Type I, II, III, or V PFD appropriately sized or a PFD of the proper buoyancy under the new system
  - Properly fitting for each person
  - In serviceable condition
- Some local government regulations require all persons to wear a PFD under certain circumstances such as: on smaller boats, at times of heightened risk, off the beach sailing yachts, sailboards, kayaks, canoes, pedal boats, etc.

- Children
  - Local regulations go even further and dictate age requirements for children to wear a PFD at all times. We recommend that right now you do an Internet search for your local government regulations for PFD requirements. In the United States and Australia, these regulations are statewide. In other countries, they are country wide
  - Your children grow. At the start of each season, or more often, make sure your children fit their PFD and the buoyancy listed is correct
  - When fitting a child's PFD, test the fit by lifting the child by the PFD at the shoulders to make sure they don't slip out
  - Make sure you always buckle the strap that passes between their legs
- Infants
  - Prior to boating with an infant, test out the fit of the selected PFD in a swimming pool. Since infants grow so fast, you should test the fit of the PFD often
  - The design should be such that the infant naturally rolls and floats face up without assistance
- Don't forget to test each PFD at the start of each season. Remember, the law says your PFDs must be in good shape before you use your boat. Ones that are not in good shape should be cut up and thrown away

Inflatable PFDs

Chances are that you will be switching over to an inflatable PFD pretty soon, especially now that we have convinced you to wear a comfortable PFD. Here the adult is wearing a 150 N inflatable PFD, while the Child is wearing a comfortable 100 N PFD.

Inflatable PFDs are life-critical, semi-complicated devices that need proper maintenance and attention. They inflate when immersed in water either by detecting hydrostatic pressure or by a pill that dissolves when it comes in contact with water. The pressure bottle that holds the compressed air can be used only once, and the mechanism that fires the pin to pierce the seal on the compressed air bottle must also be reset and replaced. Additionally, they need to be inspected annually. Beyond all that, however, once you realize how comfortable (and sometimes stylish) they are, you'll be happy you've made the transition. We have posted additional information about care and use of inflatable PFDs if you care to learn more on our blog site to the right.

Personnel Emergencies

As the skipper of a vessel, you are expected to be able to handle situations thrust upon you at a moment's notice. Many of these situations are boat-related issues, but there are also crew injury issues for which you should be prepared to assess and handle at least enough until professional assistance arrives.

Consider if you are knowledgeable enough right now to handle:

- a broken limb
- excessive bleeding
- a severe burn
- hypothermia
- dehydration
- head injury
- a diabetic with extreme low blood sugar level
- a heart attack or identify its symptoms
- extreme allergic reaction to shellfish
- severe seasickness
- alcohol, medication, or drug reaction or overdose

If you are in the slightest intimidated by any situation above, we highly recommend you take a Red Cross medical emergency class. The class is usually conducted over two evenings and deals with issues from cuts and burns to CPR. There is no substitute for being taught by a professional. There is a significant discussion of medical emergencies that are likely to occur at sea in the NauticEd Safety at Sea Course.

A Final Note: Human life is certainly the most precious entity on any sailing vessel. Preparation and knowledge of how to handle medical emergencies can make you a living hero with living friends and relatives.

Man/Crew Overboard

MOB is serious. Man/Crew Overboard (MOB) is fortunately a relatively rare occurrence, but chances are that in your sailing career it will happen. MOB means that someone has fallen off the vessel and (hopefully) is bobbing in the water as the vessel sails away. It can be life-threatening. MOB is a high-stress event, especially for the person in the water, and often the crew will panic. Even at 5 knots of speed, the distance between the MOB and the vessel increases rapidly. And given waves, it is very easy to lose sight of the person. Distance plus coldness of the water increases the chance that you might not be able to recover the person alive.

Every skipper must have a plan and practice for this eventuality. And on every outing, the skipper should brief the crew on following the skipper's command and on remaining calm in that eventuality. Next time you're out, simply throw a PFD overboard and try to recover it. You'll find that recovery is not that easy. Skippers should train spouses or regular boat buddies on the procedure to recover themselves should the skipper fall overboard.

While MOB can occur in many scenarios, it is commonly the result of someone slipping on a wet deck, equipment failure, or just not paying attention as the vessel lurches. Fast and rehearsed action is essential and can avert a real tragedy.

The key to increasing the chances of recovering your friend/family member alive is practice-practice-practice. Why would you not? And besides, practicing is actually fun.

The first order is to appoint a crewmember to keep a watch on the MOB at all times. You must say these words to the appointed watch crew member:

"No matter what happens on the boat, no matter what else is happening, no matter what anyone says, DO NOT take your eyes off the MOB even for an instant. If you do, we could lose him."

Next, you must deploy to the MOB some temporary floatation as well as a flag marker if available. Next, get a position fix: most GPS systems have an MOB button. Activate it immediately. Now you must initiate a plan for recovery.

It is also vitally important that you gain control and the attention of remaining crew. Use names of people when issuing orders and make the orders specific. For example, instead of "someone get a throw line," say "John, in the port aft lazarette, there is a long white throw line. Get it out now please."

If a child is involved and you determine it is prudent for someone to jump in, be certain that individual (often a parent) has adequate flotation to prevent a second major problem. However, concentrate on getting the boat back to the MOB position first as fast as possible.

There are many suggested strategies for recovering an MOB. Every helmsperson, vessel owner, and/or person in charge should have practiced various procedures that they can become confident with.

The biggest thing to remember as the captain and leader of the crew is to keep your crew calm. Give complete and non-confusing orders and remain calm yourself. Your crew will pick up on your confidence and follow you if they see you're in control.

Methods of Recovery

It is your call as the skipper of the vessel as to which recovery method you feel is the safest based on the conditions and your experience.

MOB Recovery with Power

MOB recovery can be safely done using engine power. Many circumstances may make it more prudent to use your engine to get back to your MOB as fast as possible, such as cold water or wave height. Even with small waves, a person can be lost in as little as a few boat lengths.

When the decision is to motor to the MOB—several precautions should be taken.

- Ensure no lines are over the side before starting the engine.
- Be especially careful of speed in approaching the MOB. Maintain steerage.
- Be aware of propeller when close to the MOB.
- The following is a diagram showing an MOB recovery, starting from a close haul point of sail where the MOB situation occurs.

1. MOB happens: Immediately announce "Man Overboard." Appoint a dedicated watch person. Get life ring and anything else that floats overboard. Hit the MOB button on your GPS. Gain control of crew.
2. Ensure no lines are overboard. Start the engine. Head into wind and begin a crash tack

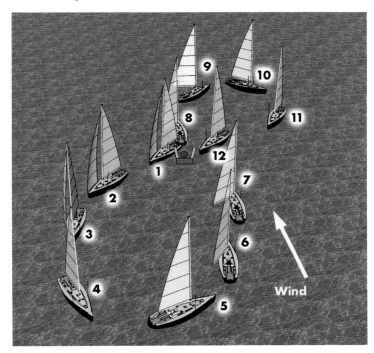

MOB. See page 174.

3.   Tighten up the main sheet. Maintain control of the crew. Act decisively with your crew. It is imperative that you lead the crew
4.   Furl or drop the headsail
5.   Head back down wind toward your MOB
6.   Get throw lines ready and cleated to the boat
7.   Communicate to the remaining crew the plan
8.   Drive the boat to a downwind position
9.   Bring the boat around
10. Ensure the boat and your crew are ready for pickup
11. Head toward your MOB from downwind
12. Bring the boat alongside to the windward side of the MOB. If you don't have a rear transom on your boat, you'll need a block and tackle, a spare halyard, or the boom topping lift to get your MOB on board. Be aware that pulling a person out of the water is virtually impossible. Your boat is equipped with all types of winches, blocks, and halyards—use them. Next time you're on your boat, plan what you would do to get a heavy person back into your boat. Buy equipment if necessary.

The Deep Beam Reach Method

The Deep Beam Reach shown in the next video is also useful for an MOB recovery when the course had been anywhere from upwind to a broad reach. It involves sailing a broad reach to a position downwind of the victim, and then tacking to make the approach upwind.

1. Bear away to a broad reach
2. Trim the mainsail, furl or drop jib
3. Tack
4. Sail a beam reach to a point slightly leeward of the victim
5. Prior to reaching the victim, depower the mainsail by letting it out and then turn upwind on to a close reach angle. Allow the boat's momentum to carry the boat to a point slightly to windward of the victim and stopping next to the victim. Be aware that the boat's momentum does not carry you past the victim. If you stop short, that's ok; you can power the mainsail slightly by bringing it in.

The Quick Stop Method

This represents the fastest means for returning to a victim, always keeping the boat relatively close by. The maneuver is exactly the same as the recovery with power method shown above, except it can be done with the engines off. View this video:

1. Immediately tack the boat
2. Begin the turn downwind; ignore jib if the crew is not available to tend
3. Continue turning to directly downwind. Ease out mainsheet
4. Sail downwind for only a boat length or two, trimming sails if possible, but not necessarily. Drop the jib if possible
5. Control the mainsheet to prepare for gybing
6. Gybe the boat
7. Sail upwind to windward of the victim. Try to angle the boat to be on a close reach at the stopping point. Luff or drop all sails

The Heave To Method

Heave to is a very effective MOB recovery method and should be considered as a first option, especially if the victim can easily swim back to the boat. Review the heave to page in Chapter 6: Sailing. When you heave to, the boat almost instantly stops dead in the water. The faster it is done, the less distance the boat gets away from the victim and often the victim is able to swim back to the boat. It requires little or no effort by the crew because the jib is left alone and only the main is let out after the boat is tacked.

More MOB Thoughts

- Ensure no lines are over the side before starting the engine
- Be especially careful of the boat's momentum in approaching the MOB Maintain steerage. Be aware of propeller when close to MOB
- Always during sailing, have lines and throwable floatation available within quick reach
- Consider specialized MOB hoisting gear when your boat does not have an easy entry transom
- Stow a change of clothes and a blanket on your boat

Final note comparing power vs. sail recovery: It is your decision on how to get back to the crew member as fast as possible depending on conditions and your ability. Some instructors teach only the sail back method because they are concerned with lines in the water getting caught in the prop. Some teach starting the engine and motor back while dousing the sails because it does not rely on your expert sailing ability to get back to your crew member in the exact right position. Some say the heave to method is the way to go. It is a contentious point among instructors.

We leave it up to you as the skipper who knows your own abilities the best. If you are not confident about sailing back, then don't (check for lines in the water before you start your engine). If you can do a heave to or a crash tack or some other method and sail back with confidence, then do that.

Electrical Emergencies

When a small keelboat vessel with an outboard engine loses DC electrical power, it is usually not a big problem unless you are sailing at night.

For this reason, it is advisable to have as an essential safety item one each of white, green, and red portable back-up navigation lights.

They are relatively inexpensive, and a quick search on Google for portable navigation light will locate them; or just visit your local chandlery, which is more than likely to have them in stock. Some have suction mounts, some have C-clamps, and some mount on the pulpit railing. Obviously, they should be stowed in an easily accessible place—AND the batteries should be checked often.

A flashlight (with operational and often-checked batteries) is also an essential electrical safety item on board.

Engine Emergencies

If your engine suddenly begins losing power and then stops altogether—you probably have a fuel flow problem.

Possible causes are:

- low fuel levels (duh)
- fuel tap is turned off (usually failure occurs within 1 to 2 minutes of starting)
- bad fuel
- poorly connected fuel hose
- the vent on the tank has not been opened (most common problem)

The engine will stop also for a few other common reasons. A line wrapped around the propeller is a very common one. In this case, the engine will start out of gear, but as soon as the engine is put into gear the engine stalls. A worse scenario is that the water impeller inside the water pump has disintegrated and the engine has overheated. This is bad—very bad! Usually, you will need a mechanic to fix this, especially if you have damaged the engine from its overheating.

Ensure you have an adequate tool kit on board including a variety of screwdrivers, pliers, wrenches, hammers, and gloves for working around a hot engine.

Most mechanical emergencies are preventable by regular scheduled professional maintenance. This will not only give the skipper peace of mind, but also save big bucks in the end and, most important, ensure joyful, safe, and efficient sailing.

Your anti-Murphy plan regarding engine failure, then, is to become adept at sailing the boat to the dock. When bringing the boat back to the marina, leave the sails in a position where they can be quickly re-hoisted if you have an engine failure.

Rigging Emergencies

Rigging emergencies seldom occur but are usually due to lack of regular inspection. At least quarterly, you should check all the cotter pins in the shackles for your standing rigging. Cotter pins prevent shackles from unwinding. Without them, a shackle can unwind in a matter of a few hours of sailing.

Fire

Putting out fires quickly is essential. The sooner the source is determined, the quicker the fire can be extinguished. Crew knowledge of the location of fire extinguishers and fire blankets is paramount. Placement of these items with large, clear signs should be carefully designed for ease and speed of access.

Many countries' laws require fire blankets to be installed on board. Law or not, fire blankets are a good idea. Fire blankets should be located near the stove and in each cabin that does not have a second egress. A fire blanket should not be mounted above the stove. This would require you to reach through the fire to access the blanket. You can use a fire blanket to throw over a fire to smother it out, or you can wrap yourself in the fire blanket to move quickly through a fire.

Prevention

On the water, fire can be the death of you and your crew. Thus, it is overly important to take all preventative measures.

Electrical

- A leading cause of electrical fire is the AC plug to the boat. It is often not secured properly and thus leads to sparks and shorts. Each time you leave the boat, make sure the AC plug is securely fastened

- Turn off nonessential electrical circuits when leaving the boat
- Ensure your boat is properly fitted with an easy-to-reach and easy-to-find switch that disconnects the batteries from the DC system. When a DC electrical fire breaks out, this switch is your first defense at extinguishing the source of the fire.

Stoves

- Turn off gas supply to cookers when not in use
- Do not leave the cooker unattended when in use
- Do not leave items close to the cooker
- Take extra caution with cooking oils and fats. Especially because the boat may be rocking
- Take extra care with children cooking

Detectors

Smoke detectors should be fitted in the main cabins and each sleeping cabin for early detection.

Gas alarm systems are an easy install on a vessel and detect LPG spilled over from the stove. Since LPG is heavier than air, it can collect in the bilges over time. If the gas alarm sounds:

- make the crew aware (called "sounding the alarm")
- turn off the LPG tank
- don't use any electrical devices
- vent the area by opening hatches
- don't activate the electric bilge pump due to electric sparks

Extinguisher Requirement

Remember, this is your life we're talking about. You spend thousands on insurance, so please invest a few extra bucks in enough proper fire extinguishers to do the job. The job being—saving your life and your beautiful boat.

Here is a recommendation on number, size, and type of extinguishers you should have on your vessel:

Boats 16 feet to less than 26 feet	Boats 26 feet to less than 40 feet
At least two type ABC-I and an ABC-II if you can fit it.	At least three type ABC-I and a couple of ABC-II if they can fit.

The letters ABC refer to the type of fire that the device is able to fight.

- A = combustible materials
- B = combustible fuels
- C = electrical

Thus, an ABC fire extinguisher is a chemical dispersion spray extinguisher and is the most commonly recommended for a boat, since it can fight all types of fires that occur on a boat. The number refers to the volume of extinguishing material contained and thus the portability (weight). Type ABC-I is a lot more portable than Type ABC-II and can thus be more time effective in the ability of the crew to get the extinguisher to the fire source. However, Type ABC-I will run out of extinguishing material faster than Type ABC-II. So it's prudent to have enough of both types on board.

Ever been to a clean bathroom in a restaurant? You can bet that they are the ones with a signed inspection routine posted on the wall. Do that to your boat—post a signed inspection sheet regarding your extinguishers. It'll impress your crew and visitors. Add a note to the bottom to say "If out of date, please inform the captain."

Set up this routine:

- Check the gauge monthly.
- For chemical types, remove and shake upside down twice a year to keep the chemicals mixed. Have the bottle weighed and professionally inspected annually.

The ultimate key in firefighting is to not hurt yourself or the crew. Be prepared to abandon ship if necessary, and let your insurance take the loss.

Sinking

A boat sits down in the water until it has displaced the same weight of water as the weight of the boat. It is a universal arrangement between boat and water. "You stay out and I will stay on top." When there is a breakdown in that boat-water agreement, a potential emergency arises.

Getting a hole in the hull (being "holed") can be minor or catastrophic. Often finding where the hole is can be a major problem. A first place to look is seacocks and sink drain pipes. The wood plugs stored in your emergency kit are used for driving into a burst seacock.

If not a seacock and you can find the hole, and you can patch it with whatever you have to stick in or cover the hole, you are probably in no danger. Most sailboats are fitted with an automatic bilge pump. These can handle small leaks, but big ones? Not so much. However, should the hole be inaccessible or too large to patch, you may have to consider using a variety of pumps, buckets, and potential abandonment.

For whatever reason, should your vessel begin taking on copious amounts of water and sinking is a possibility, you must do something fast.

Because of the many air pockets in a modern vessel, it is unlikely it will truly sink. Abandon the vessel if floating conditions of the vessel become impossible. Stay with the vessel even if it maintains minimal floating. You are more likely to be seen by rescue aircraft if you stay with the vessel.

Running Aground

In the information age, running aground is usually caused by an amateur mistake, and besides the potential damage, it is also highly embarrassing. A common error in thinking (or not thinking) is to be using an electronic chart whereby the zoom level is too far out for the screen to display a low water area.

Should the grounding cause you to be stuck, such as into a mud bottom, you may have difficulty getting off. If there is a rising tide, you may decide to wait it out. However, if the tide is going out, you need to work fast to get loose.

To get out of your predicament, use any combination of the following:

1. luff the sails to stop the driving force.
2. use the engine to try to back off.
3. if you can not back off, put the rudder and engine tiller hard over and use power to turn the boat around. It should screw around fairly easily with the keel as the pivot point.
4. heel the boat over by putting all the crew to one side. Leaving the sails up can also aid in heeling the boat. Heeling will effectively lift the keel up enough to get you unstuck.
5. Kedging: Once turned around, walk the anchor out into deeper water in the direction from where you came. Haul in on the anchor with a winch. You may need to use floatation to swim the anchor out farther.

When chartering a boat, it is prudent and ethical to report any grounding. If you've caused damage, and not reported it, you may be endangering the life of the next group who charter the boat.

Summary

Sailing emergencies are real. However, their chances of occurring are greatly diminished by obeying rules, safe practices, good maintenance behavior, and having a comprehensive knowledge base.

Preparations for emergencies come by studying and listening to those who have had emergencies. Panicky behavior is to be avoided at all times. Practice emergency situations when you are under normal conditions, especially Crew Overboard. One day it may save your friend's or family member's life.

Congratulations on working your way through this book. We really hope you enjoyed it and were able to enable the QR Codes throughout to gain a more interactive and visual appreciation of the information presented.

Visit the webpage for this book using the QR code or go to www.nauticed.org/book-sskb. There you will find any updates and other useful information.